*The Best Spiritual Reading Ever*

Also by Christopher Howse

*Best Sermons Ever* (Continuum, 2001)

# The Best Spiritual Reading Ever

Edited by

## Christopher Howse

continuum
LONDON • NEW YORK

**Continuum**
The Tower Building, 11 York Road, London SE1 7NX
370 Lexington Avenue, New York, NY 10017–6503

www.continuumbooks.com

First published 2002

**British Library Cataloguing-in-Publication Data**
A catalogue record for this book is available from the British Library.

ISBN 0–8264–6288–X

Typeset by BookEns Ltd, Royston, Herts.
Printed and bound by MPG Books Ltd, Bodmin, Cornwall

*For my parents*

# Contents

# Introduction

To settle down with a good novel or biography is to deliver oneself up to the author. If one does not trust the author one cannot lose oneself in the fiction or enter into the life as presented by the biographer. The present book is not like that. These authors are not, individually, to be trusted. They are great spiritual writers, but plain logic tells us that they contradict one another. Indeed it is, in practice, a virtue that these writers say such awkward things. They cast unexpected lights on previously familiar objects in our minds. Light from an unaccustomed angle might distort the image, but it makes us look at it again.

What, after all, would the writers here make of each other? George Fox, the Quaker (1624–91), would have fiercely denounced the liturgical ceremonies followed by Lady Lucy Herbert (1669–1744); to him a steeple-house was an abomination, popery worse, even earthly courtesy-titles an ungodly absurdity. Lady Lucy would look on Fox as a heretic for sure, a man on the side of those that had sent her recent forebears to their deaths, and if she read his journals she might take him for a lunatic. But Fox finds God's light in his own soul, just where Lucy Herbert looks in her meditations. Fox, for example, sees the words of the Virgin Mary in the gospel 'My soul doth magnify the Lord' not just as an historical utterance, dead words; they are applicable, alive and active today. Moreover Lucy Herbert took the scripture in the same way as Fox, not only to provide proof texts for doctrine, but also to speak to the reader individually.

In this I am not saying that if you take away the differences between these writers you will be left with an uncontentious teaching that everyone can swallow for nourishment. That does not work. All you would have left would be a great pile of chaff, but no grain worth the keeping. These people each lived in a system of belief; their religion was their life. Take away the living structure and the fruit is squashed and spoiled.

Anyone who uses these authors as spiritual reading will have to work in partnership with them. If you are a George Fox, accept Lucy Herbert's Mass-going; if you are a Lucy Herbert allow George Fox his rants against priests in their steeple-houses. If the meat is too strong, give it over and try the next dish. (It is to be hoped, though, that there is nothing here to give anyone food-poisoning.) As Aquinas observed, any fool can dig a hole that another man cannot fill in; anyone can raise doubts another cannot quieten. But that happens in life without having to turn to books. To put the matter solemnly, the wise reader 'is like unto a man that is an householder, which bringeth forth out of his treasure things new and old' (Matthew 13: 52).

This book is divided into three main sections, beginning with the search for God (even if it afterwards turns out that he has taken the initiative in what we thought was our search for him). Caxton's St Christopher was looking for a strong master to serve, but he eventually found a child to help. The search for God is not only for those who are yet to become Christians. The discernment of a vocation (as Benedict suggests in his description of an abbot), or shrinking from it (as Gregory warns), forms part of the Christian's journey towards God.

The second section deals with the God that is discovered: the hearing of the still, small voice; the appeal of Jesus and his Mother to mankind; through the making visible in Christ of the mysterious God who is invisible; as a consequence of the thirst that, as Julian of Norwich writes, God has to love and be loved in return.

The third section examines the response to God – primarily prayer and a new way of behaviour, both in liturgical worship and in the practice of what used (without shame) to be called virtues. In other words, perseverance in the interior life.

The very phrase 'interior life' has a technical flavour about it, as if a Christian followed a hobby, like a radio ham. But it will do to describe the hidden, sometimes incommunicable reality of relating to God. The 'interior monologue' captured by some novelists becomes for the Christian an interior dialogue, not just during periods of formal prayer but throughout the day. Those who hope to keep alive a regular habit of prayer have historically regarded spiritual reading as the intellectual food to sustain it. At the least Christians have traditionally set themselves a book or a course of reading for Lent. There are 40 divisions in this book; I know that Lent has more than 40 days, but towards the end of Holy Week, on the eve of Easter, there are plenty of other things to demand attention.

This kind of reading can also be neatly sliced into three kinds: doctrinal exposition; devotional work intended to stir up prayerful considerations; and biographies of saints. At the centre, over-lapping all three is the consideration of Jesus Christ to whom, for a Christian, implicitly, everything else is directed. It would be possible to compile a book of spiritual reading from all traditions of belief, from Animism to Zoroastrianism, but this is not it; I could not begin to judge what writings from other religions demand attention, and a pick-and-mix from world religions can easily give a very superficial, even misleading, impression of their life and thought.

I have chosen to begin Part 1 with biographical material from the journals of two people – who can say if they are saints? – in the grip of a strong and sometimes painful urge to seek a new way of life. George Fox devotes his life to seeking a new religious system; Charlotte Bedingfeld (1770–1852) has the system all right, but lacks the life. They were both experiencing a crisis of vocation: he at the beginning of his independent manhood; she apparently at the end of her social usefulness. Unlike hagiographies, their journals do

xiii

not neatly package up, for the edification of the reader, the graces granted them by God. The strange story of Charlotte Bedingfeld shows a woman frustrated almost beyond bearing by the lack of a role accorded her because she is a woman, and a widow. Her faithfulness to a life of prayer and her refusal to despair lead her at last to a way of life that brings her fulfilment, looking after children and acting as a lady-in-waiting at the royal court. Her extraordinary shuttling between a secluded convent and the worldly court of William IV gives a rare picture of the quotidian practice of a religious ideal at a period not ordinarily seen as one of Christian energy.

At the same time, journals are a borderland of literature. Are they meant to be read by the authors themselves or by posterity? But at least they come in a disguise that disarms the reader's resistance. Less beguiling are works that the eighteenth century called paraenetic and that we would call preachy. Yet among them are books that really did change people. Take William Law's *Serious Call to a Devout and Holy Life*, which came out in 1729. It exploded on that century, which from one perspective seems the tired heir of the Enlightenment, with sudden force. Even the anti-Christian Gibbon saw Law's merits: 'If he finds a spark of piety in his reader's mind, he will soon kindle it to a flame.' It found just such a spark in the mind of John Wesley, who read it when it came out and wrote in his journal: 'The light flowed in so mightily upon my soul that every thing appeared in a new view.' Under God, without Law there would have been no Methodism. At about the same time, Samuel Johnson, an undergraduate at Oxford, 'took up Law's *Serious Call*, expecting to find it a dull book (as such books generally are), and perhaps to laugh at it. But I found Law quite an overmatch for me; and this was the first occasion of my thinking in earnest of religion.' George Psalmanazar (1679–1763), the celebrated impostor, who fooled bishops and university dons into taking him for a native of Formosa, first began to think of turning to a more honest profession after being moved by Law. The power of the book persisted. A century after its publication

John Keble remarked to Hurrell Froude (1803–36): 'The other day you said that Law's *Serious Call* was a very interesting book. It was as though you had said that the Day of Judgement will be a pretty sight.' If Law does not have the same irresistible effect today (although some readers are much moved), it is partly because he so accurately put his finger on the habits of life and mind of Englishmen in the generations before the industrial revolution. That world has gone.

In any case the industrial age set the steam presses turning so fast that readers could afford to take up one cheap book and throw aside another. When Jane Austen published her novels in three volumes apiece, each volume sold for eighteen shillings – the weekly wage of an agricultural labourer. A book costing £20 at the beginning of the twenty-first century accounts for less than a twentieth of the average British weekly wage. And there are free libraries. We are surrounded by more books than we could ever read. For three-quarters of the Christian era most people read any books they could understand that were to hand, for books existed only because someone had gone to the trouble of copying out every word with a pen and ink. If you were a monk, you had access to books that had survived because they were valued enough to transcribe.

Much reading, even after the introduction of printing, was not solitary, private, visual, but public, shared, aural. Benedict, in his rule for monastic life, compiled in about the year 535, directs that there shall be reading aloud during the meals taken in common by the monks in the refectory. There is to be no whispering or verbal requests for things to be passed to the diners while the book is being read. The reader is to fulfil his duties for a week, and to be allowed a piece of bread and some wine before the meal begins, lest it be hard for him to continue fasting. He is to take his dinner after the others have finished, along with those who are serving at table that week. But unlike serving, which is to be undertaken by all the monks in turn, reading is only to be entrusted to those whose performance edifies the listeners.

There was, even so, a private aspect to monastic reading, for just as the daily work of the monk might include copying out books for the abbey library and for exchange with other monasteries, so his own spiritual life was nourished by reading to himself. (There is some debate about the practice of completely silent reading, with the eye alone; at the end of the fourth century Augustine of Hippo was surprised to find Ambrose of Milan reading a book without murmuring the words with his lips.) Lanfranc's monastic constitutions, from the eleventh century, show the annual handing in and issuing of books. Unlike the annual bath, this was obligatory, although there was no prohibition on supplementing either reading or washing in between times.

The Bible was to be read, of course, and parts of it formed the backbone of public prayer, Christian meanings growing like coral on the psalms, the poetry attributed to David the shepherd-king of Israel. The first Christians sang psalms; later, a monk on entering a monastery would after a little time come to know by heart the psalms he recited at periods each day; the Book of Common Prayer (from the time of its first compilation in the sixteenth century) divides the 150 psalms so that they can be gone over every month. A metrical version of the psalms in English was contrived for public recitation by Thomas Sternhold (1500–49) and John Hopkins (who died in 1570). It was criticized for its bad style and inaccuracy, but through its repetition people learned the psalms. The same thing happened with the metrical version that supplanted theirs, the work of Nicholas Brady (1659–1726) and Nahum Tate (1652–1715). (In New England the Bay Psalm Book of 1640 informed a whole tradition of Puritanism.) Tate certainly had a populist touch. He was the author of 'While shepherds watched their flocks by night' and 'improved' Shakespeare, partly by supplying happy endings to his tragedies.

Since in this book there are no passages taken from the Bible (which is taken as read), there are no psalms; a comparison of translations would make a book in itself. If the psalms fed private prayer because they had been learned by heart, the same was true of hymns. Thomas More joked with his family that if they were reduced to beggary they could go from door to door singing the *Salve Regina* for alms. The same song had been sung each Saturday on deck by Columbus's men on their voyage into the unknown West. Nearly 400 years later, Bishop William Bernard Ullathorne, the bluff, reforming Yorkshireman, heard, from his ship coming home from Australia, the same song sung by slaves returning from the fields in Brazil. The music made it easier to remember, just as it does the *Ave Stella Maris* of Monteverdi, the chorales of Bach or Isaac Watts's 'O God, our help in ages past' (loosely based on Psalm 90). In fact well-loved hymns often have no great poetic merit; their power comes from being known by heart and summoning up deeply felt connections with weighty themes, at best between creature and Creator.

The great bulk of spiritual reading feeds prayer in a different way, not by bringing to mind phrases from a vocabulary of prayer but by providing insights or prompting feelings, affections, movements of the heart that would never have occurred otherwise. Some people take a book with them when it is time to settle down and pray, for they have learned by experience that at that particular time either they will be unable to think of anything at all connected with God, or they will have their best intentions drowned out by trivial distractions – the shopping list, or what to say to the boss at work. Teresa of Avila, that honest and practical woman, found that she was unable to pray on her own without being prompted by a book for a period of many years. Later, the opposite problem prevailed; as she says in her *Spiritual Testimonies*: 'I read very little, because in picking up a book I become recollected in my contentment, and so the time for reading passes in prayer.'

When Teresa said, as she often did in her autobiographical writings, that she was not one of the *letrados*, she only meant that she was not one of the learned in the law and academic theology. (Anyway, she often used her protestations as a means of deflecting criticism of her active role as a woman in a society dominated by men.) She did not mean that she was illiterate. She relied on a book to teach her about the life of prayer during a period when she had no reliable human adviser. She knew enough Latin for her public prayers, but could not follow it in an unfamiliar book. Historically Christianity and literacy have gone together. Before many years had passed, the first Christians were circulating the letters of Paul and copying out the gospel accounts of the life of Jesus. The early generations of Christians made strenuous efforts to preserve the purity of the written texts of what we now call the New Testament, and there were fierce debates over which writings were to be considered canonical.

There was room, though, for writings that no one claimed as inerrantly inspired. An early historical work such as the *Acts of Polycarp* (from about AD 156) supplied the common requirements of a spiritual work, for it recounted the holy life, and more importantly the holy death, of the Bishop Polycarp, invited a prayerful reaction to it, and implicitly provided a theological pattern for the behaviour of his contemporaries and later generations.

More systematized theology came from a man whom Polycarp had taught: Irenaeus. He took on the task of explaining why the heterodox gnostics were wrong in their teachings, and contrariwise how authentic Christianity, deriving from the original followers of Jesus, could be explained coherently. To summarize the view of Irenaeus given by Rowan Williams in 1979 (in his book *The Wound of Knowledge*), the gnostics rejected the value of Jesus Christ having come in the flesh; to them the limitations of bodily human nature were to be escaped by applying information, *gnosis*, a sort of formula that was guaranteed to be effectual. Irenaeus had a difficult path to tread of presenting an intellectual demonstration of why an intellectual salvation was not enough; for it was what Jesus *did* that availed, and Christians, through communion with the person of Jesus, were to share in his personal relation with God the Father. Jesus is the new Adam, who mends the human race that Adam marred, and so, as Irenaeus put it in *Adversus Haereses*: 'In the human race are brought to perfection the mysteries of God which the angels long to see.'

Fortunately, Christianity, while stressing that what really mattered was loving rather than knowing, avoided despising intellectual efforts to clarify its own doctrine. It is true that the theology of the so-called *via negativa* asserts that God is unknowable. This strand of thought came to be caught up permanently with the practice of mystical prayer through a very curious accident of history. From the sixth century onwards, some tracts on the nature of God were circulated under the name Dionysius the Areopagite. This is the man mentioned in the Acts of the Apostles (Chapter 17) as one of the people of Athens who accepted Paul's preaching. The Areopagite had not in fact written these, much later, tracts, but he was generally thought to be the author. And so his ideas were taken with much greater seriousness than would otherwise have been the case. Indeed he is the non-scriptural authority most commonly quoted by Thomas Aquinas (1225–74) in his great *Summa Theologiae*. Writers on prayer discovered, in the teachings of the pseudo-Dionysius that God was utterly incomprehensible to the human mind, a very useful explanation of a common phenomenon. This phenomenon is that after persevering for a good time in daily prayer, men and women found that the activity of prayer itself became dry or distasteful to them, and that, though they held on to God by faith, there were really no words, or even ideas, that could express the way in which the deepest part of their hearts, minds or souls apprehended God. This aspect of mental prayer, some would say mystical prayer, can be traced through the centuries in the writings of great mystics like John of the Cross, whose 'Dark Night' expresses the sometimes painful inadequacy of the soul that bares itself to the contemplation of God. Since such matters are by their nature not susceptible to concrete language, fierce controversy has never been far from their expression in written form.

It is striking that a tradition of mystical writing on prayer, influenced by pseudo-Dionysius but derived far more from personal experience, can be traced through English writers, certainly from the fourteenth century, with the writings of Richard Rolle and Walter Hilton. The anonymous author of another fourteenth-century work, *The Cloud of Unknowing*, also rendered into English a short work by the pseudo-Dionysius under the title *Hid Divinity*. A commentary on this is to be found in the voluminous works of the seventeenth-century Welshman living in exile, Augustine Baker (1575–1641). Baker's most influential book (actually an edited extract compiled posthumously) was *Sancta Sophia* (Holy Wisdom). This contained such profitable material that it used to be read annually by the English Benedictine abbot Cuthbert Butler (1858–1934), according to David Knowles. Knowles himself, whose own life may be described as tragic in the strict sense of the word, had his differences with Augustine Baker, although it must be pointed out that in Knowles's day far less of Baker's work was available in a form that presents his position fairly. But the underlying teaching – that prayer depends on persevering faith in God and that inexpressible prayers are produced in the human soul by the work of the Holy Spirit – is returned to by a living writer in the Carmelite tradition of John of the Cross and Teresa of Avila: Ruth Burrows (born 1924).

This selection is meant to be Anglocentric. By this I mean that the examples are either from English-language writers or from authors that were familiar in the central tradition of spirituality in the English-speaking world. Sometimes this tradition has been surprisingly resistant to sectarian differences. The *Imitation of Christ*, for example, was written by a Catholic in the Low Countries in the fifteenth century; a manuscript copy, written (perhaps sixteen years after its first composition) by Thomas à Kempis himself, is dated 1441, while the earliest surviving manuscript copy of it written in England is dated 1438, three years earlier than that autograph version. Certainly it had been translated into English by the mid-fifteenth century. It weathered the Reformation, was meditated upon by John Wesley, and, by the time it was packed into knapsacks for the trenches of the First World War, in pocket editions, rubbing against the New Testament, the Book of Common Prayer and Coverdale's translation of the Psalms, the *Imitation* was almost assumed to be an English book. Similarly the Calvinism of Bunyan was ignored by generations of Anglican readers, at least as far as *Pilgrim's Progress* was concerned, as it went through endless illustrated parlour editions or was given away as a school prize. No one would have dreamed of sending Bunyan to jail for that.

On the whole I have avoided very well-known passages. An exception is Augustine's celebrated psychological and theological analysis of his boyhood theft of pears. Here the translation is that of Abraham Woodhead (1609–78), not because it is uniquely stylish or accurate, but because its unfamiliar language allows the incident to be read anew. In any case, translation of an ancient author is an impossible problem; nineteenth-century translations make them sound schoolbookish or parsonical, but present-day versions disguise the very difference of the author's cultural presuppositions from our own. Perhaps the most artificial style included in this book is Thomas Browne's. He achieves his baroque plate-spinning masterfully; it is not mere euphuism, bombast and lacquer. He never uses a strange word without making its meaning clear in the context. Grotesqueness of language is not the idea; caesura and momentum drive the reader on. He has learnt from his predecessors when an oddity will work. It is the lesson taught by Robert Southwell, who described Mary Magdalen's grieving for Jesus in these terms: 'Hee was her only Sunne, whose going downe left nothing but a dumpish night of fearefull fancies.' Or John Donne who, in order to make his own image Christ's, invites God to 'burne off my rusts', as if he were repainting iron railings.

Richard Crashaw's poem on a prayer book to be carried in the bosom of the recipient is almost shocking in its accommodation of the language of light, idle, romantic love to the love of God. At first the reader is tempted to reject Crashaw's assumption that swooning raptures have anything to do with the Christian way. It seems to fit as badly as Bernini's statue of St Teresa in an apparently only too physical ecstasy. But really Crashaw is subverting not Christianity but the language of sexually romantic poets by stealing their elevated ideal of undying love and applying it to a love that in truth outlasts mortal life.

Not that sexual imagery need have shocked a pre-Renaissance reader. Bernard of Clairvaux (1090–1153) wrote a commentary on the Song of Solomon that is a classic of mystical insight. But it depends on the literal meaning of the Old Testament book as a sexual love poem. And a fifteenth-century Christian accustomed to invoking the Virgin Mary as *hortus conclusus*, an enclosed garden, would be not at all surprised by the Jungian interpretation of the garden in men's dreams as an image of the female body. It would too be a daring or unwise writer in our own day who would go as far as the holy mystical writer Julian of Norwich in depicting Jesus as a mother to us spiritually, suckling as we do, in a way, on the blood and water flowing from his wounded side.

Meditation in the form of verse also managed to find a readership that bridged the divides of Christianity after the Reformation. As Louis Martz points out in his foreword to the *Poems of Edward Taylor* (Yale, 1960), this late seventeenth-century American Calvinist stood in the same tradition as the sixteenth-century English Jesuit poet Robert Southwell. Between the two come John Donne (1572–1631) Catholic turned Protestant, angel of the pulpit and metaphysical poet; George Herbert (1593–1633), the ideal of an Anglican clergyman; and, again, Richard Crashaw (1613–49), forced abroad following his conversion to Catholicism.

The great prose influence on Taylor's generation, both in Britain and America, was the nonconformist Richard Baxter (1615–91), author of *The Saints' Everlasting Rest* (1650). His people, he says, do not know what meditation is, so busy are they running from sermon to sermon. 'They have thought that meditation is nothing but the bare thinking on Truths, and the rolling of them in the understanding and memory' – which indeed, in this vigorous language, sounds a good start. He has in mind something like John Henry Newman's distinction between the notional and the real. As Baxter puts it:

O how easily may they be deceived here, while they do nothing more than reade of Heaven, and study of Heaven, and preach of Heaven, and pray, and talk of Heaven? What, is not this the Heavenly life? O that God would reveal to our hearts the danger of this snare! Alas, all this is but mere preparation: This is not the Life we speak of, but it is indeed a necessary help thereto. I entreat every one of my brethren in the Ministry that they search and watch against this Temptation: Alas, this is but gathering the materials and not the erecting of the building itself.

Baxter is a hard taskmaster. Francis de Sales (1567–1622), in his *Introduction to the Devout Life* and *The Love of God*, is just as convinced of the importance of erecting the building itself, but he makes it sound pleasant, like bees building a honeycomb or birds a nest. He, like Thomas à Kempis, found a place in the hearts of English-speaking people. John Henry Newman put up prints of scenes from his life around the little altar set up in his room at the Oratory in Birmingham.

I have tried to avoid controversialist prose in this selection. Otherwise I would have included some of the writings of James I (VI of Scotland). But just when he is getting on nicely in construing the Lord's Prayer or whatever, his King Charles's head (to speak anachronistically) pops up and he is denouncing the Pope as Antichrist or fuming against purgatory. Thomas More can be tiresome in the opposite direction, particularly when filleting dull books by now forgotten opponents. And I would like to have included the strange tales *Illustrious Providences* by the New England Puritan Increase Mather, if he did not continually use them as a divine stick to beat the Quakers.

Still, an historical approach has strong advantages. I have supplied a little more biographical material for some less familiar figures than for the Queen Elizabeths of history. In their lives and writings we find that present-day concerns are not the only ones that have a claim to be placed in the foreground. At other times we are surprised by how like us figures from hundreds of years ago can be. The anonymous fourteenth-century author of *The Cloud of Unknowing* clearly found that luggage from past failings could be discouraging, as many do today.

More than that, the authors here often have breathtaking insights, or sharp analyses, or write in a style that makes their prose pleasurable whatever they say. It would be possible to read most of these writers without sharing their religious beliefs, just as we can enjoy a performance of the *Bacchae* without worrying whether the god Dionysius really exists. Thomas Traherne's catalogue of praise and thanksgiving for the body would give pleasure to a pantheist. But to read Donne or Anne Bradstreet without sharing their belief in the Resurrection or heaven would be to add a tragic element to art that already bears the poignancy of human transience. The Christianity that informs the readings in this book does not nullify suffering and sorrow, but it gives hope with what is unmistakably good news.

# PROLOGUE

## *The point of reading*

# The lover's book
# Richard Crashaw

*Richard Crashaw (1613–49) was happy as a Cambridge don until the chapel of Peterhouse was sacked in the Civil War and he was expelled with other fellows who would not take the Parliamentary Oath. He had been a friend of Nicholas Ferrar who set up a systematically Christian way of life at Little Gidding, which Crashaw often visited before Ferrar's death in 1637. Crashaw had early success with a volume of sacred Latin epigrams. His English verse uses daring conceits in the 'metaphysical' manner, as here, where the conventions of romance are applied to the love of God.*

**On a prayer-book sent to Mrs M. R.**

Lo, here a little volume, but great book
(Fear it not, sweet,
It is no hypocrite),
Much larger in itself than in its look.

It is, in one rich handful, Heaven, and all
Heaven's royal hosts encamp'd, thus small;
To prove that true schools use to tell,
A thousand angels in one point can dwell.

It is love's great artillery,
Which here contracts itself, and comes to lie
Close couch'd in your white bosom, and from thence,
As from a snowy fortress of defence,
Against the ghostly foe to take your part,
And fortify the hold of your chaste heart.

It is the armoury of light;
Let constant use but keep it bright,
You'll find it yields,
To holy hands and humble hearts,

3

More swords and shields
Than sin hath snares, or hell hath darts.

Only be sure
The hands be pure
That hold these weapons, and the eyes
Those of turtles, chaste and true,
Wakeful and wise.
Here is a friend shall fight for you,
Hold but this book before your heart,
Let prayer alone to play his part.
But oh! the heart
That studies this high art,
Must be a sure house-keeper,
And yet no sleeper.

Dear soul, be strong,
Mercy will come ere long,
And bring her bosom full of blessings,
Flowers of never-fading graces;
To make immortal dressings
For worthy souls whose wise embraces
Store up themselves for him, who is alone
The spouse of virgins, and the Virgin's son.

But if the noble Bridegroom when he comes
Shall find the wand'ring heart from home,
Leaving her chaste abode,
To gad abroad
Amongst the gay mates of the god of flies
To take her pleasures, and to play
And keep the devil's holy day;
To dance in the sunshine of some smiling
But beguiling
Sphere of sweet and sugar'd lies,

Some slippery pair,
Of false, perhaps as fair,
Flattering but forswearing eyes;

Doubtless some other heart
Will get the start,
And stepping in before,
Will take possession of the sacred store
Of hidden sweets and holy joys,
Words which are not heard with ears,
(These tumultuous shops of noise)
Effectual whispers, whose still voice
The soul itself more feels than hears.

Am'rous languishments, luminous trances,
Sights which are not seen with eyes,
Spiritual and soul-piercing glances,
Whose pure and subtle lightning flies
Home to the heart, and sets the house on fire,
And melts it down in sweet desire
Yet doth not stay
To ask the windows' leave to pass that way.

Delicious deaths, soft exhalations
Of soul! dear, and divine annihilations!
A thousand unknown rites
Of joys, and rarified delights.

An hundred thousand loves and graces,
And many a mystic thing,
Which the divine embraces
Of th' dear spouse of spirits with them will bring,
For which it is no shame,
That dull mortal'ty must not know a name.

Of all this hidden store
Of blessings, and ten thousand more;
If when he come
He find the heart from home,
Doubtless he will unload
Himself some other where,
And pour abroad
His precious sweets
On the fair soul whom first he meets.

O fair! O fortunate! O rich! O dear!
O happy and thrice happy she
Dear silver-breasted dove
Whoe'er she be,
Whose early love
With winged vows,
Makes haste to meet her morning spouse,
And close with his immortal kisses;
Happy soul who never misses,
To improve that precious hour:
And ev'ry day,
Seize her sweet prey,
All fresh and fragrant as he rises,
Dropping with a balmy shower
A delicious dew of spices.

Oh I let that happy soul hold fast
Her heavenly armful; she shall taste
At once ten thousand paradises;
She shall have power,
To rifle and deflower
The rich and roseal spring of those rare sweets,
Which with a swelling bosom there she meets,
Boundless and infin'te, bottomless treasures
Of pure inebriating pleasures,

Happy soul, she shall discover,
What joy, what bliss,
How many heavens at once it is,
To have a God become her lover.

# The year's book
# Lanfranc

*Lanfranc (1005–89) became Archbishop of Canterbury in 1070. He had been born in Pavia and became a Benedictine monk at Bec. His own* Monastic Constitutions *sketch out a humane, regular life for men dedicated to prayer. For them, reading was to inform their minds and feed their spiritual life.*

On the first Sunday of Lent the invitatory shall be sung by two in albs. After Compline a curtain shall be hung between the choir and the altar.

On Monday before Terce the crucifix, hanging circlets and reliquaries, and gospel books with images upon them, shall be covered.

Before the brethren go in to chapter, the librarian should have all the books save those that were given out for reading the previous year collected on a carpet in the chapter-house; last year's books should be carried in by those who have had them, and they are to be warned by the librarian in chapter the previous day of this.

The passage from the Rule of St Benedict concerning the observance of Lent shall be read, and when a sermon has been made on this the librarian shall read out a list of the books which the brethren had the previous year. When each hears his name read out he shall return the book which was given to him to read, and anyone who is conscious that he has not read in full the book he received shall confess his fault prostrate and ask for pardon. Then the aforesaid librarian shall give to each of the brethren another book to read, and when the books have been distributed in order he shall at that same chapter write a list of the books and those who have received them.

# PART 1

# *The Search for God*

# 1

# Youthful zeal
# George Fox

*George Fox (1624–91) founded the Society of Friends, or Quakers as others called them. He was the son of a prosperous puritan weaver and had been intended for the Church of England ministry. But when George was still eighteen, the incident below, recounted in his* Journal, *set him seeking another way. Imperceptibly, Fox's quest became a mission. He felt driven by God to preach eternal truth, which he thought was 'infallibly' guaranteed by an inner light.*

*Fox wrote, or dictated, the* Journal *towards the end of his life. He had been imprisoned eight times (once for three years); he had refused to doff his hat to any authority; he travelled to every corner of Britain and drew hundreds to the Society of Friends, though their meeting houses were shut up or demolished and the worshippers jailed.*

*Here he is looking back at a time before the Friends were gathered together. He calls churches 'steeple-houses'; he refuses to refer to the days of the week or the months of the year by their ordinary names; by 'professor' he means someone who calls himself a Christian.*

When I came towards nineteen years of age, being upon business at a fair, one of my cousins, whose name was Bradford, a professor, and having another professor with him, came to me and asked me to drink part of a jug of beer with them, and I, being thirsty, went in with them; for I loved any that had a sense of good, or that sought after the Lord. When we had drunk each a glass, they began to drink healths, calling for more, and agreeing together, that he that would not drink should pay all. I was grieved that any who made profession of religion, should do so. They grieved me very much, having never had such a thing put to me before, by any sort of people; wherefore I rose up to go, and putting my hand into my pocket, laid a groat on the table before them, and said, 'If it be so, I will leave you.'

So I went away; and when I had done what business I had to do, I returned home, but did not go to bed that night, nor could I sleep, but sometimes walked up and down, and sometimes prayed and cried to the Lord, who said unto me, 'Thou seest how young people go together into vanity, and old people into the earth; thou must forsake all, both young and old, and keep out of all, and be as a stranger unto all.'

Then at the command of God, on the ninth day of the seventh month, 1643, I left my relations, and broke off all familiarity or fellowship with old or young.

I passed to Lutterworth where I stayed some time; and thence to Northampton, where also I made some stay; then to Newport-Pagnell, whence, after I had stayed a while, I went to Barnet, in the fourth month, called June, in 1644. As I thus travelled through the country, professors took notice and sought to be acquainted with me; but I was afraid of them, for I was sensible they did not possess what they professed.

Now during the time that I was at Barnet, a strong temptation to despair came upon me. Then I saw how Christ was tempted, and mighty troubles I was in; sometimes I kept myself retired in my chamber, and often walked solitary in the chase, to wait upon the Lord. I wondered why these things should come to me; and I looked upon myself and said, 'Was I ever so before?' Then I thought, because I had forsaken my relations, I had done amiss against them; so I was brought to call to my mind all the time that I had spent, and to consider whether I had wronged any. But temptations grew more and more, and I was tempted almost to despair; and when Satan could not effect his design upon me that way, he laid snares for me, and baits to draw me to commit some sin, whereby he might take advantage to bring me to despair.

I was about twenty years of age when these exercises came upon me; and I continued in that condition some years, in great trouble, and fain would have put it from me. I went to many a priest to look for comfort, but found no comfort from them ...

About the beginning of the year 1646, as I was going to Coventry, and approaching towards the gate, a consideration arose in me, how it was said that 'all Christians are believers, both Protestants and Papists'; and the Lord opened to me that, if all were believers, then they were all born of God, and passed from death to life, and that none were true believers but such; and though others said they were believers, yet they were not.

At another time, as I was walking in a field on a first-day morning, the Lord opened to me, 'that being bred at Oxford or Cambridge was not enough to fit and qualify men to be ministers of Christ'; and I wondered at it, because it was the common belief of people. But I saw it clearly as the Lord opened it to me, and was satisfied, and admired the goodness of the Lord who had opened this thing unto me that morning.

But my relations were much troubled that I would not go with them to hear the priest; for I would get into the orchards, or the fields, with my Bible by myself. I asked them: Did not the apostle say to believers, that 'they needed no man to teach them, but as the anointing teacheth them'? And though they knew this was Scripture, and that it was true, yet they were grieved because I could not be subject in this matter, to go to hear the priest with them. I saw that to be a true believer was another thing than they looked upon it to be; and I saw that being bred at Oxford or Cambridge did not qualify or fit a man to be a minister of Christ: what then should I follow such for? So neither these, nor any of the Dissenting people, could I join with, but was as a stranger to all, relying wholly upon the Lord Jesus Christ.

At another time it was opened in me, 'That God, who made the world, did not dwell in temples made with hands.' This at first seemed a strange word, because both priests and people used to call their temples or churches, dreadful places, holy ground, and the temples of God. But the Lord showed me clearly, that he did not dwell in these temples which men had commanded and set up, but in people's hearts: for both Stephen and the apostle Paul bore testimony, that he did not dwell in temples made with hands, not even in that which he had once commanded to be built, since he put an end to it; but that his people were his temple, and he dwelt in them ...

After this, I met with a sort of people that held women have no souls (adding in a light manner), no more than a goose. But I reproved them, and told them that was not right; for Mary said, 'My soul doth magnify the Lord, and my spirit hath rejoiced in God my Saviour.'

Now though I had great openings, yet great trouble and temptation came many times upon me; so that when it was day, I wished for night, and when it was night, I wished for day ... I fasted much, and walked abroad in solitary places many days, and often took my Bible, and went and sat in hollow trees and lonesome places till night came on; and frequently, in the night, walked mournfully about by myself for I was a man of sorrows in the times of the first workings of the Lord in me.

During all this time I was never joined in profession of religion with any, but gave myself up to the Lord, having forsaken all evil company, and taken leave of father and mother, and all other relations, and travelled up and down as a stranger in the earth, which way the Lord inclined my heart; taking a chamber to myself in the town where I came, and tarrying sometimes a month, more or less, in a place; for I durst not stay long in any place, being afraid both of professor and profane, lest, being a tender young man, I should be hurt by conversing much with either. For which reason I kept myself much as a stranger, seeking heavenly wisdom and getting knowledge from the Lord; and was brought off from outward things, to rely wholly on the Lord alone. Though my exercises and troubles were very great, yet were they not so continual but that I had some intermissions, and was sometimes brought into such a heavenly joy, that I thought I had been in Abraham's bosom. As I cannot declare the misery I was in, it was so great and heavy upon me; so neither can I set forth the mercies of

God unto me in all my misery. O, the everlasting love of God to my soul, when I was in great distress! when my troubles and torments were great, then was his love exceedingly great.

At another time I saw the great love of God, and I was filled with admiration at the infinitude of it; I saw what was cast out from God, and what entered into God's kingdom; and how by Jesus, the opener of the door, with his heavenly key, the entrance was given; and I saw death, how it had passed upon all men, and oppressed the seed of God, in man, and in me; and how I in the seed came forth, and what the promise was to. Yet it was so with me, that there seemed to be two pleading in me; questionings arose in my mind about gifts and prophecies; and I was tempted again to despair, as if I had sinned against the Holy Ghost. I was in great perplexity and trouble for many days; yet I gave up myself to the Lord still.

One day when I had been walking solitarily abroad, and was come home, I was wrapped up in the love of God, so that I could not but admire the greatness of his love. While I was in that condition it was opened unto me by the eternal Light and Power, and I saw clearly therein, 'that all was done, and to be done, in and by Christ; and how he conquers and destroys this tempter, the Devil, and all his works, and is above him; and that all these troubles were good for me, and temptations for the trial of my faith, which Christ had given me'. The Lord opened me, that I saw through all these troubles and temptations; my living faith was raised, that I saw all was done by Christ, the Life, and my belief was in Him. When at any time my condition was veiled, my secret belief was stayed firm, and hope underneath held me, as an anchor in the bottom of the sea, and anchored my immortal soul to its Bishop, causing it to swim above the sea, the world, where all the raging waves, foul weather, tempests, and temptations are ...

There was a great meeting of professors, and a captain, whose name was Amos Stoddard, came in. They were discoursing of the blood of Christ; and as they were discoursing of it, I saw, through the immediate opening of the Invisible Spirit, the blood of Christ.

15

And I cried out among them, and said, 'Do ye not see the blood of Christ? See it in your hearts, to sprinkle your hearts and consciences from dead works, to serve the living God': for I saw it, the blood of the New Covenant, how it came into the heart. This startled the professors, who would have the blood only without them, and not in them. But Captain Stoddard was reached, and said, 'Let the youth speak; hear the youth speak': when he saw they endeavoured to bear me down with many words ...

We had great meetings in those parts, for the power of the Lord broke through in that part of the country. Returning into Nottinghamshire, I found there a company of shattered Baptists, and others; and the Lord's power wrought mightily, and gathered many of them. Afterwards I went to Mansfield and thereaway, where the Lord's power was wonderfully manifested both at Mansfield and other neighbouring towns. In Derbyshire the mighty power of God wrought in a wonderful manner. At Eaton, a town near Derby, there was a meeting of Friends, where there was such a mighty power of God that they were greatly shaken, and many mouths were opened in the power of the Lord God. Many were moved by the Lord to go to steeple-houses, to the priests and to the people, to declare the everlasting truth unto them ...

I saw the state of those, both priests and people, who, in reading the Scriptures, cry out much against Cain, Esau, and Judas, and other wicked men of former times, mentioned in the Holy Scriptures; but do not see the nature of Cain, of Esau, of Judas, and those others, in themselves. These said, it was they, they, they, that were the bad people; putting it off from themselves; but when some of these came, with the light and Spirit of truth, to see into themselves, then they came to say, I, I, I, it is I myself that have been the Ishmael, and the Esau, etc. For then they came to see the nature of wild Ishmael in themselves; the nature of Cain, of Esau, of Korah, of Balaam, and of the son of perdition in themselves, sitting above all that is called God in them ...

On a certain time, as I was walking in the fields, the Lord said unto me: 'Thy name is written in the Lamb's book of life, which was

16

before the foundation of the world'; and, as the Lord spoke it, I believed, and saw it in the new birth. Then, some time after, the Lord commanded me to go abroad into the world, which was like a briery thorny wilderness; and when I came, in the Lord's mighty power, with the word of life into the world, the world swelled, and made a noise like the great raging waves of the sea. Priests and professors, magistrates and people, were all like a sea, when I came to proclaim the day of the Lord amongst them, and to preach repentance to them.

I was sent to turn people from darkness to the light, that they might receive Christ Jesus: for, to as many as should receive him in his light, I saw that he would give power to become the sons of God; which I had obtained by receiving Christ. I was to direct people to the Spirit, that gave forth the Scriptures, by which they might be led into all truth, and so up to Christ and God, as they had been who gave them forth. I was to turn them to the grace of God, and to the truth in the heart, which came by Jesus; that by this grace they might be taught, which would bring them salvation, that their hearts might be established by it, and their words might be seasoned, and all might come to know their salvation nigh. I saw that Christ died for all men, and was a propitiation for all; and enlightened all men and women with his divine and saving light; and that no one could be a true believer, but who believed in it. I saw that the grace of God, which bringeth salvation, had appeared to all men, and that the manifestation of the Spirit of God was given to every man, to profit withal.

These things I did not see by the help of man, nor by the letter, though they are written in the letter, but I saw them in the light of the Lord Jesus Christ, and by his immediate Spirit and power, as did the holy men of God, by whom the holy Scriptures were written. Yet I had no slight esteem of the holy Scriptures, but they were very precious to me, for I was in that Spirit by which they were given forth; and what the Lord opened in me, I afterwards found was agreeable to them. I could speak much of these things, and many volumes might be written, but all would prove too short to set forth the infinite love, wisdom, and power of God, in preparing, fitting, and furnishing me for the service he had appointed me to; letting me see the depths of Satan on the one hand, and opening to me, on the other hand, the divine mysteries of his own everlasting kingdom.

Now, when the Lord God and his son Jesus Christ sent me forth into the world, to preach his everlasting gospel and kingdom, I was glad that I was commanded to turn people to that inward light, Spirit, and grace, by which all might know their salvation, and their way to God; even that Divine Spirit which would lead them into all truth, and which I infallibly knew would never deceive any.

# Zaccheus
# Christopher Smart

*Christopher Smart (1722–71) excelled as a poet while still an undergraduate and then as a fellow of Pembroke Hall (as it was still called), Cambridge. He later lived as a periodical writer. He is remembered for the surviving fragments of his* Jubilate Agno, *and for being mad, which led to periods of confinement in the Bethlehem Hospital (Bedlam). Later he was detained for some months in the King's Bench prison, and its liberties, for debt.*

**The Story of Zaccheus**

> Through Jericho as Jesus came
> A man (Zaccheus was his name)
> Chief of the Publicans for gold
> And pow'r, sought Jesus to behold;
> But could not for the press his eyes
> Indulge by reason of his size.
> He therefore hasty ran before,
> And climb'd upon a sycamore,
> That he his passing Lord might see,
> Who when he came beside the tree,
> Look'd up, and saw him o'er his head
> 'Zaccheus, haste, come down,' he said;

'For in thy house this very day
Thy Lord has purposed to stay.'
He therefore coming down in haste,
with joy his holy Guest embrac'd
Which when observ'd by all the rest,
They murmur'd, that he went a guest
With one so much immers'd in sin.
Mean time Zaccheus stood within,
And said unto the Lord, 'Behold,
The half of my ill-gotten gold
I give the poor; and if by theft,
Or falsehood, any I've bereft,
Four-fold the same I will replace.'
Then answer'd Jesus: 'This day grace
Is come upon this house; for he
Is also Abraham's progeny.'

*Praise-worthy in a high degree*
*Is godly curiosity;*
*To search the Lord, above, around,*
*If haply he may yet be found.*
*Short-sighted reason, dwarf desire,*
*Are faith and zeal when lifted high'r.*
*Then on the Tree of Life sublime*
*With hands and knees devoutly climb;*
*Catch mercy's moments as they fly,*
*Behold! the Lord is passing by.*

# 2

# Restlessness in old age
# Charlotte Bedingfeld

*The cultural circumstances of Charlotte Bedingfeld (1770–1852) could hardly have been more different from those of George Fox. She was born into the old Suffolk Roman Catholic family of Jerningham and at the age of fourteen went to school at an Ursuline convent in Paris. In 1795 she married Sir Richard Bedingfeld of the romantically castellated Oxburgh Hall, Norfolk, although they were obliged to live for some time at Ghent to save money.*

*Lady Bedingfeld was sincerely pious, but in the 1820s she suffered a succession of grievous blows: the deaths of her two brothers and their wives, of her favourite daughter and a son, drowned at sea, of her mother, and in 1829, of her husband of 34 years. She was left without a role and retired to a convent at Hammersmith, renting a room the walls of which she covered with portraits of her beloved family.*

*There she kept a journal remarkable for its honesty in contemplating the annoyances of daily life and the hopelessness of her prospects, until she entered into a final, unlooked-for, period of valued work.*

*Monday 22 February 1830* The Abbess, to my painful Surprise did not come to see me at her usual time before my Dinner. I felt almost inclined to be hurt! What unreasonable beings are we! As if she could know of what Value her visit is to me – and why it is of such Value I cannot tell.

The Dinner was gloomy. Mrs Adlerkrone, terribly low, and talking of her complaints in an alarming manner; she was lamenting that Mrs Rieman was going to a party and deprecating the Idea of being all alone at Supper. I felt so sorry for her that I said: 'No you shall not be alone, I will come down.' She caught my hand eagerly and kissed it, expressing her gratitude. Her state is most painful to witness.

When I went to my room, I had a visit from Mr Biddulph. He had a message to the Abbess. I sent for her, wondering what she would say about not coming in the Morning. She said nothing – only: 'How have you been all day?' Mr B. had a Mind to see the Chapel so she took us into the Quire and from there I led him down into the Chapel, and so to the Door, and returned to my room, thinking how Exigeante I was, and that of course the Abbess could not go on coming to see me every day.

In the middle of these thoughts she entered and then said her Brother from the North had come to see her in the Morning, just as she was coming to me. I felt pleased at that Explanation and shewed her a Letter I had had from my daughter the Nun and some old Letters. She staid with me till her Supper time, 5 o'clock.

When dusk came on and I could not see to do anything, all my Melancholy came over me and every thing else was forgotten – I laid down on my Sofa, and wept.

After a time the Servant brought the Lamp and the tea things and I revived, drank tea and wrote to Constance Clifford; there was no Complin, but at 8, I went down according to promise and staid till 9. Poor Mrs Adlerkrone was sadly agitated, and while she was cutting her Bread with the Dinner knife I almost felt afraid of what might ensue if her Malady increased in the Smallest degree. She was difficult about her supper, and visibly wretched. She says that she cannot read or apply her mind to anything, that everything is 'swept out of her Mind' – that it is 'empty like an unfurnished house'; and if she did not offer up prayers continually, the Devil might take possession of it. I was glad when the Lay sister came in and said it was 9 o'clock.

*Tuesday 23 February* Pretty well all day. Mrs Adlerkrone was very much agitated at Dinner, her Speech was affected as if she had an impediment, like stuttering, and spoke in such a low tone of voice . . .

*24 February* Ash Wednesday. Very nervous. Went to first Mass – and just as I was watching to go to the 2nd at the right moment, my Nephew Edmund Jerningham arrived. I regretted leaving him, but could only shake hands and obey the summons of the Bell. I was anxious to do what had been told me, about the ceremonial of the Ashes, and I felt uneasy about the Abbess, who could not go on with the prayers: after the 1st Mass her Voice failed her from weakness, which it seems it often does when fatigued.

According to directions I followed the Pensioners to the Chapter House where we all sat very quietly till their Mistress summoned them (the Community having all received Ashes) to enter the Quire. I followed and Mr Bellisent, having duly crossed our foreheads with them at the Quire rails, went down to the Chapel and we went to our usual places.

The Abbess came at her usual hour, but I could perceive an alteration in the tone of her Voice, higher and weaker. She only laughed and said it was often so after a long Office; she eats scarcely anything, I am told, and of course must be very weak. I feel quite Uncomfortable about her. How much wiser it is to care about nobody! But then again, how insipid every place would be! There would be no amusement but eating and drinking!

Mrs Adlerkrone did not appear at Dinner but is not worse. The Abbess came to me again after her Supper, if Supper it was! And told me she was not going to the Evening Office, which I was glad of, though it is a certain sign that she feels worn out.

*Friday 26 February* Mrs Adlerkrone was in better spirits at Dinner and in a Complimentary Mood; she annoyed me extremely by extolling 'My powers of Conversation', etc., etc. Poor little quiet Mrs Rievnan added her puff of incense! I am not however much elated with being the first in this trio. In a beleaguered town, hunger makes all food palatable, and so is my conversation.

I walk in the garden in the Evening; there was something very soothing to me in the Weather, still and grey, and fresh – like subdued sorrow. The Abbess and Mother Prioress were each walking up and down (separately) the long gravel walk. I had Godefridus, which greatly helped to elevate my mind. I felt it, however, rather embarrassing to pass the Abbess without any mark of recognition, and took refuge in the farther garden, but there it was rather damp.

*Tuesday 2 March* A Night of less Sleep than Usual. Awake by 6. The Weather very close; but one Mass, which I was glad of for I felt as if I could hardly kneel. The Abbess came rather later than usual, which curtailed her Visit. I abstain from Butter at Breakfast, though I eat as much as I can of a French roll. For the first time I begin to believe that dry Bread is less nourishing than when accompanied with Butter, for notwithstanding I seem to swallow as much solid Bread as I did before Lent, I feel a painful Sickness by 12 o'clock, and it hinders me from enjoying the only sunshiny hour of the day, that of the Abbess's Visit. I have leave not to fast but I wish to make a difference.

I get tired of the Dinner business. Mr Bellisent dined out; he does not converse much, but his countenance is sensible and he serves as a poise to my very flighty companion, Mrs Adlerkrone. After Dinner I returned to my room, and my Spirits gave way. I went into the lower Chapel at 4 for the Litany and Complin. I hoped to be alone, but I found the Pensioners there: it seems they come to the Litany in Lent. I out-staid them some time, shedding many tears. When I thought The Nuns were gone to supper, I ventured forth to the bottom of the garden, but it felt damp and I dared not stay – I returned to my room and rang for my tea. I took up Godefridus; but I could not check my tears.

The Abbess arrived and it roused me. It was almost dark, I know not if she could see my countenance, her conversation had its usual effect and I am now much better. I take nothing to eat at tea, but save the piece of my Morning roll to eat, with a glass of water before I go to bed. It is two hours to tea, and I begin to feel faint; and my bit of roll is very small, for I was obliged to take a piece of it at 12.

*Wednesday 3 March* A day without tears, but not more comfortable on that account. The Revd Mr Wilde, the 'extraordinary' [i.e. a priest who was not the ordinary chaplain], came to hear all the confessions, and the Abbess had settled the day before that I should go to him in her room, when summoned, perhaps at 11, perhaps at 12. This made me feel quite sick and nervous. A little after 12, a Lay Sister (whom I don't know) came with the Message that Dame Catherine [a nun] was with him and that my Lady said I was to follow. I placed myself on my knees in my little dark passage, with the Door ajar from which I could command a view of the other doors. I perceived various Sisters and Pensioners in the Abbess's Cell, I felt sick with Nervousness and a fear of not hearing when this Dame C would come out, though 5 steps from me.

Mr Wilde I found very pleasing and holy, but I felt hurried, knowing so many wanted to go. I was glad when I got safe back into My room and shut the door.

I wrote a great deal, and prepared for Communion. I went to Bed but had a very disturbed Night, and every time I began to fall asleep I was roused by a knock, seemingly upon the chest of Drawers close to my Bed. I felt surprised but not alarmed, the Idea of Ghosts has long ceased to terrify me! Many times have I lain, looking about my room, at the dead of night, and wishing to see the dear well-remembered forms of those who have disappeared for ever! I had a light in my room and could conceive no cause for these little knocks. They were exactly as if somebody had knocked with their knuckle at my door, or rather on the drawers by the Bedside. Whatever it was, I answered it with a prayer! It occurred 4 times; every thing in the house was perfectly still, above and below, but the house dog bark.

*Saturday 7 March* In the Morning, Lady Bradford came near 3 and staid till past 4. We had a long and melancholy conversation. As she is fond of Nuns, and partial in all to the Catholic Religion, I asked for the Abbess. She came and conversed some time and when she was gone, Lady B. said she thought she was very pleasing. I shewed her the Quire and chapel, and our dining room. She found it more like a Convent than she had expected, being so near London.

There is something in the Strict Order and Control of a Religious House which is wise and Salutary. I should never have gained so much ground in the ways of Resignation elsewhere. One of the most agonizing feelings attached to the loss I have sustained is the dreary Independence it bestows! At least, it is so to me. My disposition has always found it pleasanter, in all the daily arrangements of life (as relating to myself), to follow rather than to lead. This made me, I suppose, feel such deference for my Parents, such affectionate respect for my higher Relations, Uncles, etc., etc., and for aged people in every rank of life. To those who feel in this particular as I do, Time not only afflicts but terrifies by removing what we leaned upon for Security!

The Convent Life, conceals this. Wherever there are permissions and prohibitions and Limits, and fixed hours and control there is Protection implied, and that sweet word brings back the recollection of Youth and Childhood, and all its blessed Ignorance and Security!

This reluctance to advance in years grew with my growth and seemed to augment as my mind opened. While Pensioner in the Convent of the Ursuline Nuns at Paris, I enjoyed every moment; the only thought that saddened my buoyant spirits was the sudden recollection sometimes that I was almost 'grown up' and must soon go forth into the world.

My next dread was Marriage. Admirers, I thought, were things of course, but would have wished to treat them as in the days of Chivalry; their approbation I tolerated, and Lances might be broken in honour of me if I could be left unspoken to with my Parents. Time and with it some increase of Wisdom sobered my high spirits and I entered on a new Era. I commenced a happy married life; so happy that I used to wonder why this world was called the 'Valley of Tears'!

But I still felt the dread of advancing in my career. Each year, as it closed, was regretted as a friend departed for ever, and the new one was hailed with something of the fear and Mistrust which attends the first meeting with a new Master: how will he treat me?

I have now survived my domestic happiness! He who constituted it is gone! My Parents are no more! Of my Uncles, I have but one left! Of three Brothers but one! Of my Sisters-in-law, but one! And of those dear ones who call me Mother, two are gone! What then makes me wish to linger behind? The same dread of change! The same clinging to what is the same attachment to persons and places?

*The volume of Charlotte Bedingfeld's journal for 1831 finds her outer life transformed by her appointment as Woman of the Bedchamber to Queen Adelaide, wife of William IV, whom she had met years before at Ghent. Now she is quite equal to the physical demands of court life, but continues to retire to the still life at the convent.*

*Thursday 28 April 1831* Drawing room crowded, 12.00. Stood on the 2nd Step of the throne behind the Duke of Leeds. We were a great many in attendance. Lasted about 2 hours and a half. The Queen told me she had put something round her knee, to lessen the fatigue of bending it so often.

*Friday 29 April* Returned to the Convent, felt tired but not so low as usual, nothing can exceed Edmund Jerningham and his pretty Wife's attention to me.

My head has been very heavy and uncomfortable, feeling very desolate, My motive, my Spring for action! broken! Nothing left but Self, tired-out self! The Sight of relatives and friends rouses me, and my Natural Spirits rise to the top, but when again alone, how heavily they sink again to the bottom! If I had everything at will, I could not invent a life, or rather a manner of living, that could fill the Void and make me happy. But I can be merry sometimes, and that must do. If it pleased God that I had stronger health I might walk about, and do some good to my Neighbour as in former days, but that Comfort is denied me, and I am thrown back on Self, odious Self!

*9 May* Miss Langton brought Lady Harriet Murray to see me, she is daughter to Lady Rothes (in her own right) who married a Gardener. I thought I saw it in her daughter's face, a Vulgar-looking little person, but not so in manner. She is married to Mr C. Murray, a Lawyer, the son of a Man with one Leg, that Used to be a great playfellow of Mine, when very Young at Cossey. I remember he cried most bitterly when I went over to the Convent in Paris, and I have never met with him since!

Very low almost all day.

*12 May* Drawing-room, weather fine, felt better, very full attendance. The Princess Louisa sat down, which I thought a great liberty; when Mr Talleyrand passed, he had some minutes very serious whispering conversation with her! Lady Gore said to me: 'Look there, when those two whisper there is Mischief brewing!' and then added, laughing, 'Whenever I see Talleyrand I expect to smell Sulphur and Brimstone.' He appears universally abhorred.

The King looked pale and harassed, the Queen as usual. When we took leave in the King's Closet, she said to me in French: 'Ma Soeur arrive avec ses enfants Mercredi; je voudrais vous envoyer à sa rencontre, soyez ici à midi.'

I am to proceed in one of her Carriages to meet the Duchess at the Tower Stairs: she comes with 6 Children.

I got back to the Convent about 5. The Nuns all very curious to see me. It is a new thing for one belonging to the household to lodge in a Convent.

*From 1831 until 1833 the books are missing. The last surviving volume is labelled: 'Windsor Castle, Autumn, 1833'.*

*1833* I went down to Windsor on third of August. I had an Apartment on a level with the Corridor, the first door past the Royal Staircase. A grand Military dinner in St George's Hall.

*20 August* Epsom Races. Accompanied their Majesties, went in a carriage with Lady Falkland, Miss Wilson and Col. Bowater. Rather a tedious day, the races following each other very Slowly. The Queen had her work, so shall I, if it happens again.

We were in a very handsome tent or room; between this temporary building and the course there was a space occupied by the Servants, which prevented the people coming too near. I suppose the Insult, or rather danger, which the good king incurred last year, caused this arrangement.

*Wednesday 27 August* Attended the Queen to London, as Lady in Waiting. Our horses were the Queen's and a *relais* halfway. I looked with pleasure at the little humble convent door as we passed through Hammersmith.

Grand dinner at St James's. I was going to place Myself at the end of the table with Lord Albemarle when I heard my name and, looking up, saw the Duke of Cumberland, beckoning me to come by him and the Queen smiling and making me a Sign to the same effect. I obeyed though rather dreading that his Royal H. was going to be teasing and disagreeable. The Queen says I am a favourite of his, because (says he) I Understand a Joke! He administered one to me during dinner, which I parried as well as I could. I am generally inspired with a saucy reply, which I suppose amuses him.

*Thursday 19 September* I attended the King and Queen to a farewell Dinner at Kew, to the Duke and Duchess of Cumberland; went alone with Col. Bowater in a Coach and four. The Queen took no others of the household, as the Duke of C.'s dining room is not very large. Col. Bowater is a worthy kind-hearted man, and we talked the whole way there and back without weariness. He told me that his father being an Admiral, he had begun by the Sea, and sailed in the same Ship as his father, who never spoke to him, or saw him oftener than his fellow Midshipmen, and this was such a painful restraint to him, afflicted him so much, that he begged to return to School. He said he had been most fortunate through Life. It is refreshing to My Spirits to meet with anyone who is Satisfied with his Lot, and grateful to his Benefactors.

*Saturday 28 September* The Queen at Breakfast was seized with Lumbago; she was in great pain, but laughed at it. However, the intended excursion to Kew was put off and the Queen appeared no more that day. It was my Lot to be led to Dinner by his Majesty, and of course sat next to him and Lady Taylor on the other side. There were no guests but Mr Spring Rice and Colonel Campbell. I asked the King who that 'handsome man' was, adding I thought, but I ought not perhaps to say so, that he was like my family. The King said: 'Why not? Yours is a beautiful family.'

After dinner, I sat at the Queen's table with the King and Lady Falkland. His Majesty called Mr Spring Rice and made him Sit down on the Sofa where the Q. usually sits, and talked a great deal to him, seeming amused. Mr Spring Rice is very lively, expresses himself well, and seems to see everybody and everything *en couleur de rose*. I was glad to hear him; many clever people have a vein of discontent or Satire running through them which tinges every account they give. He had probably not been in contact with royalty before, and was visibly elated.

*Here ends the last surviving fragment of Charlotte Bedingfeld's journals. She continued to spend her existence, oddly, yet seemingly with peace and comfort to herself, between the two extremes, Windsor Castle and the Hammersmith Convent, until the Queen's death in 1849, three years before her own.*

# Jesus sought
# Francis Quarles

*Francis Quarles (1592–1644) set out to become a religious versifier by writing a biblical paraphrase called* A Feast of Wormes *set forth in a* Poeme of the History of Jonah *(1620), but he succeeded beyond expectation with his* Emblems *(1635), poems to go with a series of drawings capable of figurative explanation. There had been emblem books before, and more than half of the volume was copied, pictures and all, from a book by a Jesuit, Hermann Hugo, published in Antwerp in 1624.*

*In the* Emblems, *Quarles appends a quotation and an epigram to each poem, in order to illuminate the subject. In this instance he quotes from Anselm's* Proslogion.

*Although Quarles was regularly republished for three centuries, often without illustrations, contemporary critics found his work flawed. He enjoyed images that sometimes verged on the absurd, as with the consideration below. But there is no denying that he is arresting.*

### 'By night on my bed I sought him whom my soul loveth; I sought him, but I found him not.' (Canticles 3.1)

The learned Cynic having lost the way
To honest men, did, in the height of day,
By taper-light, divide his steps about
The peopled streets, to find this dainty out,
But fail'd: the Cynic search'd not where he ought;
The thing he sought for was not where he sought.
The wise men's task seem'd harder to be done;
The wise men did by star-light seek the Sun,
And found: the wise men search'd it where they ought;
The thing they hoped to find was where they sought,
One seeks his wishes where he should; but then
Perchance he seeks not as he should, nor when.
Another searches when he should; but there
He fails; not seeking as he should, nor where.
Whose soul desires the good it wants, and would
Obtain, must seek where, as, and when he should.
How often have my wild affections led
My wasted soul to this my widow'd bed,
To seek my lover, whom my soul desires!
 (I speak not, Cupid, of thy wanton fires:
Thy fires are all but dying sparks to mine;
My flames are full of Heav'n, and all divine.)

How often have I sought this bed by night,
To find that greater by this lesser light
How oft have my unwitness'd groans lamented
Thy dearest absence! Ah! how often vented;
The bitter tempests of despairing breath,
And toss'd my soul upon the waves of death!
How often has my melting heart made choice
Of silent tears (tears louder than a voice)
To plead my grief, and woo thy absent ear
And yet thou wilt not come, thou wilt not hear.
Oh, is thy wonted love become so cold?
Or do mine eyes not seek thee where they should?
Why do I seek thee, if thou art not here?
Or find thee not, if thou art ev'rywhere?
I see my error; 'tis not strange I could not
Find out my love; I sought him where I should not.
Thou art not found on downy beds of ease;
Alas! thy music strikes on harder keys:
Nor art thou found by that false feeble light
Of nature's candle; our Egyptian night
Is more than common darkness; nor can we
Expect a morning but what breaks from thee.
Well may my empty bed bewail thy loss,
When thou art lodged upon thy shameful cross:
If thou refuse to share a bed with me,
We'll never part, I'll share a cross with thee.

## From Anselm's *Proslogion*

Lord, if thou art not present, where shall I seek thee absent? If
everywhere, why do I not see thee present? Thou dwellest in light
inaccessible; and where is that inaccessible light? Or how shall I
have access to light inaccessible? I beseech thee, Lord, teach me to
seek thee, and show thyself to the seeker; because I can neither
seek thee, unless thou teach me; nor find thee, unless thou show
thyself to me: let me seek thee in desiring thee, and desire thee in

31

seeking thee: let me find thee in loving thee, and love thee in finding thee.

**Epigram**
> Where should thou seek for rest, but in thy bed?
> But now thy rest is gone, thy rest is fled:
> 'Tis vain to seek him there: my soul, be wise;
> Go ask thy sins, they'll tell thee where he lies.

3

# The state we're in
# Joseph Butler

*Joseph Butler (1692–1752) finds his way into dictionaries of quotations for his words in 1739, as Bishop of Bristol, to John Wesley, whose public meetings had been accompanied by strange outbreaks of emotion, cries and falling. 'Sir, the pretending to extraordinary revelations and gifts of the Holy Ghost is a horrid thing, a very horrid thing.'*

*Butler can be contrasted with his contemporary William Law as a much cooler writer, yet Butler's book* The Analogy of Religion, Natural and Revealed, to the Constitution and Course of Nature, *which came out in 1736, seven years after Law's* Serious Call, *had its own far-reaching effect. In a rational age it proceeded with logical care in great rolling periods of prose. It had a profound influence a century later on John Henry Newman, and Gladstone completed the task of editing a collection of Butler's works.*

*Butler, like Law, was the son of a well-to-do tradesman, one of eight children of a draper of Wantage, Berkshire. His family were dissenters and he was educated at a nonconformist school at Tewkesbury, Gloucestershire. But Butler conformed to Anglicanism in time to go up to Oxford and take orders. A quirk in his nature led him to undertake building work at the places he held livings. As Bishop of Bristol, the least profitable see in England, he could not make ends meet, and he often held more than one benefice. He was always moved to give to beggars, but, unlike Law, knowing his weakness, he would hide in his house if they called.*

*Joseph Butler declined the Archbishopric of Canterbury in 1747, apparently remarking that 'it was too late for him to try to support a falling church'; but he accepted Durham in 1750, dying two years later.*

There is not, I think, anything relating to Christianity which has been more objected against than the mediation of Christ, in some or other of its parts. Yet, upon thorough consideration, there seems nothing less justly liable to it. For,

I   The whole analogy of nature removes all imagined presumption against the general notion of a mediator between God and man. For we find all living creatures are brought into the world, and their life in infancy is preserved, by the instrumentality of others: and every satisfaction of it, some way or other, is bestowed by the like means. So that the visible government, which God exercises over the world, is by the instrumentality and mediation of others. And how far his invisible government be or be not so, it is impossible to determine at all by reason. And the supposition, that part of it is so, appears, to say the least, altogether as credible as the contrary. There is then no sort of objection, from the light of nature, against the general notion of a mediator between God and man, considered as a doctrine of Christianity, or as an appointment in this dispensation: since we find by experience, that God does appoint mediators, to be the instruments of good and evil to us; the instruments of his justice and his mercy. And the objection here referred to is urged, not against mediation in that high, eminent, and peculiar sense, in which Christ is our Mediator; but absolutely against the whole notion itself of a mediator at all.

II   As we must suppose that the world is under the proper moral government of God, or in a state of religion, before we can enter

33

into consideration of the revealed doctrine concerning the redemption of it by Christ; so that supposition is here to be distinctly taken notice of. Now the divine moral government which religion teaches us implies that the consequence of vice shall be misery, in some future state, by the righteous judgement of God. That such consequent punishment shall take effect by his appointment, is necessarily implied. But, as it is not in any sort to be supposed, that we are made acquainted with all the ends or reasons for which it is fit future punishments should be inflicted, or why God has appointed such and such consequent misery should follow vice; and as we are altogether in the dark how or in what manner it shall follow, by what immediate occasions, or by the instrumentality of what means; there is no absurdity in supposing it may follow in a way analogous to that in which many miseries follow such and such courses of action at present; poverty, sickness, infamy, untimely death by diseases, death from the hands of civil justice. There is no absurdity in supposing future punishment may follow wickedness of course, as we speak, or in the way of natural consequence from God's original constitution of the world; from the nature he has given us, and from the condition in which he places us: or in a like manner, a person rashly trifling upon a precipice, in the way of natural consequence, falls down; in the way of natural consequence, breaks his limbs, suppose; in the way of natural consequence of this, without help perishes.

Some good men may perhaps be offended with hearing it spoken of as a supposable thing, that the future punishments of wickedness may be in the way of natural consequence: as if this were taking the execution of justice out of the hands of God, and giving it to nature. But they should remember, that when things come to pass according to the course of nature, this does not hinder them from being his doing, who is the God of nature: and that the scripture ascribes those punishments to divine justice which are known to be natural; and which must be called so, when distinguished from such as are miraculous. But after all, this supposition, or rather this way of speaking, is here made use of only by way of illustration of the subject

34

before us. For since it must be admitted, that the future punishment of wickedness is not a matter of arbitrary appointment, but of reason, equity, and justice; it comes, for ought I see, to the same thing whether it is supposed to be inflicted in a way analogous to that in which the temporal punishments of vice and folly are inflicted, or in any other way. And though there were a difference, it is allowable, in the present case, to make this supposition, plainly not an incredible one; that future punishment may follow wickedness in the way of natural consequence, or according to some general laws of government already established in the universe.

III    Upon this supposition, or even without it, we may observe somewhat, much to the present purpose, in the constitution of nature or appointments of Providence: the provision which is made, that all the bad natural consequences of men's actions should not always actually follow; or that such bad consequences, as according to the settled course of things, would inevitably have followed, if not prevented, should, in certain degrees, be prevented. We are apt presumptuously to imagine, that the world might have been so constituted as that there would not have been any such thing as misery or evil. On the contrary we find the Author of nature permits it: but then he has provided reliefs, and in many cases perfect remedies for it, after some pains and difficulties: reliefs and remedies even for that evil which is the fruit of our own misconduct; and which, in the course of nature, would have continued, and ended in our destruction, but for such remedies. And this is an instance both of severity and of indulgence, in the constitution of nature. Thus all the bad consequences, now mentioned, of a man's trifling upon a precipice, might be prevented. And though all were not [prevented], yet some of them might [be], by proper interposition, if not rejected: by another's coming to the rash man's relief, with his own laying hold on that relief, in such sort as the case required. Persons may do a great deal themselves towards preventing the bad consequences of their follies: and more may be done by themselves, together with the assistance of others, their fellow-creatures; which assistance nature requires and prompts us to. This is the general constitution of the world. Now suppose it had been so constituted that, after such actions were done as were foreseen naturally to draw after them misery to the doer, it should have been no more in human power to have prevented that naturally consequent misery, in any instance, than it is in all; no one can say, whether such a more severe constitution of things might not yet have been really good. But, that, on the contrary, provision is made by nature, that we may and do, to so great degree, prevent the bad natural effects of our follies; this may be called mercy or compassion in the original constitution of the world: compassion, as distinguished from goodness in general. And, the whole known constitution and course of things affording us instances of such compassion, it would be according to the analogy of nature, to hope that, however ruinous the natural consequences of vice might be, from the general laws of God's government over the universe; yet provision might be made, possibly might have been originally made, for preventing those ruinous consequences from inevitably following: at least from following universally, and in all cases.

Many, I am sensible, will wonder at finding this made a question, or spoken of as in any degree doubtful. The generality of mankind are so far from having that awful sense of things which the present state of vice and misery and darkness seems to make but reasonable that they have scarce any apprehension or thought at all about this matter, any way and some serious persons may have spoken unadvisedly concerning it.

But let us observe, what we experience to be, and what, from the very constitution of nature, cannot but be the consequences of irregular and disorderly behaviour – even of such rashness, wilfulness, neglects as we scarce call vicious. Now it is natural to apprehend that the bad consequences of irregularity will be greater in proportion as the irregularity is so. And there is no comparison between these irregularities, and the greater instances of vice, or a dissolute profligate disregard to all religion, if there be any thing at all in religion. For consider what it is for creatures, moral agents, presumptuously to introduce that confusion and misery into the kingdom of God which mankind have in fact introduced; to blaspheme the Sovereign Lord of all; to contemn his authority; to be injurious, to the degree they are, to their fellow-creatures, the creatures of God.

Add that the effects of vice in the present world are often extreme misery, irretrievable ruin, and even death. And upon putting all this together, it will appear that as no one can say in what degree fatal the unprevented consequences of vice may be, according to the general rule of divine government; so it is by no means intuitively certain how far these consequences could possibly, in the nature of the thing, be prevented, consistently with the eternal rule of right, or with what is, in fact, the moral constitution of nature. However, there would be large ground to hope that the universal government was not so severely strict but that there was room for pardon, or for having those penal consequences prevented. Yet:

IV  There seems no probability, that any thing we could do would alone and of itself prevent them: prevent their following, or being inflicted. But one would think, at least, it were impossible that the contrary should be thought certain. For we are not acquainted with the whole of the case. We are not informed of all the reasons which render it fit that future punishments should be inflicted: and therefore cannot know whether any thing we could do would make such an alteration, as to render it fit that they should be remitted. We do not know what the whole natural or appointed consequences of vice are; nor in what way they would follow, if not prevented: and therefore can in no sort say, whether we could do any thing which would be sufficient to prevent them. Our ignorance being thus manifest, let us recollect the analogy of nature or providence. For, though this may be but a slight ground to raise a positive opinion upon in this matter; yet it is sufficient to answer a mere arbitrary assertion, without any kind of evidence, urged by way of objection against a doctrine the proof of which is not reason but revelation. Consider then: people ruin their fortunes by extravagance; they

37

bring diseases upon themselves by excess; they incur the penalties of civil laws, and surely civil government is natural; will sorrow for these follies past, and behaving well for the future, alone and of itself prevent the natural consequences of them? On the contrary, men's natural abilities of helping themselves are often impaired: or if not, yet they are forced to be beholden to the assistance of others, upon several accounts, and in different ways: assistance which they would have had no occasion for, had it not been for their misconduct; but which, in the disadvantageous condition they have reduced themselves to, is absolutely necessary to their recovery and retrieving their affairs.

Now since this is our case, considering ourselves merely as inhabitants of this world, and as having a temporal interest here, under the natural government of God, which however has a great deal moral in it: why is it not supposable that this may be our case also in our more important capacity, as under his perfect moral government, and having a more general and future interest depending? If we have misbehaved in this higher capacity and rendered ourselves obnoxious [vulnerable] to the future punishment which God has annexed to vice: it is plainly credible that behaving well for the time to come may be – not useless, God forbid – but wholly insufficient, alone and of itself, to prevent that punishment; or to put us in the condition, which we should have been in, had we preserved our innocence.

And though we ought to reason with all reverence, whenever we reason concerning the divine conduct: yet it may be added, that it is clearly contrary to all our notions of government, as well as to what is, in fact, the general constitution of nature, to suppose that doing well for the future should, in all cases, prevent all the judicial bad consequences of having done evil, or all the punishment annexed to disobedience. And we have manifestly nothing from whence to determine in what degree and in what cases reformation would prevent this punishment, even supposing that it would in some. And though the efficacy of repentance itself alone to prevent what mankind had rendered themselves obnoxious to, and recover what they had forfeited, is now insisted upon, in opposition to Christianity: yet, by the general prevalence of propitiatory sacrifices over the heathen world, this notion, of repentance alone being sufficient to expiate guilt, appears to be contrary to the general sense of mankind.

Upon the whole, then: Had the laws, the general laws of God's government, been permitted to operate, without any interposition in our behalf, the future punishment, for ought we know to the contrary or have any reason to think, must inevitably have followed, notwithstanding any thing we could have done to prevent it.

# Terra incognita
# Hannah More

*Hannah More (1745–1833) was intelligent and as a young woman took the opportunity of mixing with the 'blue-stockings' of London and the eminent men of their circle, including David Garrick (who called her 'Nine', as embodying all the muses) and Samuel Johnson. In her early twenties she had accepted an offer of marriage from a man twenty years her elder, who tagged her along for six years and then broke off the engagement; he did at least leave her £1,000.*

*Hannah More supported herself by writing, having a runaway bestseller in 1809 with* Coelebs in Search of a Wife *(later parodied in Captain Marryat's* Caleb in Search of a Father*). She took up with Wilberforce, opposed slavery, and joined forces with the Clapham sect around Zachary Macaulay (the historian's father) as an exponent of evangelical Christianity. In 1811 she published the successful* Practical Piety; or the Influence of the Religion of the Heart on the Conduct of Life, *from which the passage here is taken.*

We are told that it is the duty of the Christian to 'seek God'. We assent to the truth of the proposition. Yet it would be less irksome to corrupt nature, in pursuit of this knowledge, to go a pilgrimage to distant lands, than to seek him within our own hearts. Our own heart is the true *terra incognita*; a land more foreign and unknown to us than the region of the polar circle: yet that heart is the place in which an acquaintance with God must be sought. It is there we must worship him, if we would worship him in spirit and truth.

4

# Good sought in sin
# Augustine of Hippo

*Augustine of Hippo (354–430) had an extraordinarily energetic and fruitful mind. His influence on Christianity was thoroughgoing and permanent. His autobiographical* Confessions *have always been popular.*

*He was a rhetorician by training and wrote good Latin. The seventeenth-century translation here, by Abraham Woodhead (1609–78), of the famous incident of the theft of pears (rendered 'apples' by Woodhead), is not particularly good, but its very crabbedness can, in a short passage, help the reader get at what the saint is trying to analyse: his own yearning for God while he fell into sin, the parody of goodness.*

Near a vineyard of ours, there was a Tree well loaden with apples, not much tempting either sight or taste: a company of wicked Boyes of us went late at night to rob it; having till then (according to a loose custome) drawn out our sports in the streets. And thence, we carried great loads, not for our own eating, but even to be cast to the hogs, after we had first only tasted them, and delighted our selves in the doing of what we pleased, not what we ought.

Lo: my heart (O my God) lo, my heart (where of thou hadst pity, in the bottom of this hell) let it now tell thee, what it was that it then affected. Even, that I might be wicked *gratis*; and have no provocation to ill but the evil it self. I was enamoured of this, I only loved to perish; I loved to be faulty; not that thing in the which I was faulty, but the very faultiness I loved. Unclean and filthy soul, starting from thy stable firmament, toward all extremes not by a disgrace prosecuting something else, but only the disgrace.

There is a tempting appearance in all fair and glittering bodies, in gold, and in silver, and the rest: also in carnal touches, there is sympathy that transports us; and in the rest of our senses, there is a cotemperature of other Bodies exactly tuned to the complacency of each of them. Even temporal Honour, and the power of conquering and mastery, hath its splendour and ornament, whence springs so strong an appetite of revenge (yet therefore may not we for gain of these, O Lord, depart from thee, nor turn aside from thy Law). The mortal Life also which we live here hath its blandishments, from a certain kind of symmetry and proportion that it hath to all the rest of these lower beauties. And, in it, the Friendship also of Men is, in a ravishing manner, sweet from a combined union of hearts.

And, upon occasion of all these and the like, much sin is committed: whilst, by an immoderate propension to these, the last of goods, those best and highest are deserted, even Thou, O Lord our Lord, and Thy Truth, and Thy Law. For these things below have also their Delights, but not like my God, by whom all they were made, *because in him doth the Righteous delight, and he is the joy of the upright in Heart.*

Therefore, when we question, for what cause any crime is done; 'tis presumed to proceed either from a desire of acquiring, or a fear of losing, some of these the meanest of Goods: because they also are some way lovely and pretty, though in comparison to those superior treasures and beautiful riches contemptible and base.

One man hath murdered another; what moved him to it? He loved his wife, or his land, or would rob him of his own livelihood; or from the other feared some such loss; or, first injured, thirsted for revenge. Would he commit a murder upon no cause, taken only with the murder? Who can imagine this? For, as for that furious and cruel man, Catiline, that was said to be *gratuito malus atque crudelis*; spontaneously wicked, and blood-thirsty *gratis*; yet is there a cause assigned, *ne per otium*, etc., lest his mind or hand, through idleness, should grow useless. And why indeed was he such? But that the City being surprized by his mischievous practices, he might possess the honour, wealth, command thereof; that, in so necessitous a fortune and so guilty a Conscience, he might be free from fear of laws and of want. Therefore was not Catiline himself in love with his own villanies, but with something else, for which sake he did them.

But, O, my Theft, that wicked night-exploit of my sixteen year's age, what was it then that wretched I so much loved in thee? For nothing fair thou wert because thou wert Theft, or indeed wert thou at all any thing that thus I speak unto thee? Indeed the fruit we robbed was fair because it was thy Creature, thou fairest of all, Creator of all, my good God. God my true and my supreme good, fair was the fruit, but that was not it after which my miserable soul lusted, having thereof far better in great plenty of our own. But I got the other rather, because so I might steal it; which fruit being once gathered, as having now sufficiently satisfied my appetite, I threw it away; enjoying thereof only the pleasure of the sin; or, if I chanced to taste any of the fruit, that which sweetened it unto me was the offence.

And now, O Lord my God, fain would I know what it was in this fault that so much delighted me: and behold I cannot find the least allurance of any beauty in it.

I do not mean such beauty as is seen in the divine habits of Justice and Prudence;

or, as in the highest faculties of Understanding and Memory;
as in the subtility of the Senses;
or yet in the vigours of Vegetation;
nor yet (inferior to these) as the Stars are glorious and orderly in their Orbs;
or, as the Earth and Sea are beautiful in their kind; being always

laden with breed; a new growth of which in their unexhausted womb still succeeds a former departed.

But I mean such a gloss at least, as there is (a faint and painted one) in many a deluding Vice.

For, both the sin of Pride (to be some way like unto thee) emulates highness; whenas indeed thou art only, above all, the God most high:

And Ambition aims at glory and honour; whenas thou alone are honourable supremely and eternally glorious:

And the Cruelty of the great ones desires so to become reverenced and feared; and *who indeed is to be feared but God alone?* from whose power what, or when, or where, or how, or by whom, can ever any thing by force or fraud be subducted?

And the caresses of the lascivious seek to be loved; whenas neither is any thing so dearly sweet as thy *Love*, nor so savingly enamouring as thy above-all beautiful and enlightening *Truth*:

And Curiosity makes semblance of a desire of knowledge; whenas it is Thou that perfectly understandest all things.

Also, even Ignorance and folly clothes it self with the name of simplicity and innocency; because not any thing is found like simple as thy self: and, what is there innocent like thee, whose works are harmless only to the sinner.

And Sloth affects, as it were, quiet; but what repose certain besides the Lord? Luxury desires to be called satiety and plenty; yet thou are the only fulness and never-failing abundance of uncorrupting dainties.

Lavishing hides it self under the shadow of liberality; but the most royally overflowing donor of all good things is thy self.

Avarice would have much to be in its fruition; and it is thou that possessest all things.

Envy contends for pre-eminence; and what is so pre-excellent as thy self? Anger pretends just vengeance; and who executes it righteously like thee?

Fear abhors things unusual, surprizing, and Enemies to what she

43

loves, whilst she is always precautelous [careful]of her safety; now to Thee only it is that nothing comes unacquainted or sudden; and who can part what thou lovest from thee; and where, but with thee, ever dwells unshaken security?

Sorrow pines for those things lost in whose enjoyment she delighted, because she desires that nothing may be taken away from her; as nothing can, from thee. After these, the soul goes a-whoring, when she is departed from thee; and seeks, besides thee, what she never finds pure and clear, but when she is returned unto thee.

And yet all they (in a wrong way) imitate, and seek likeness unto, thee, who render themselves far from thee and who pride themselves most against thee: And, in this their imitating and resembling thee, shew thee to be the Creator of all Nature; and that in it they cannot any whither recede from thee.

What therefore in that Theft was it, that I loved? and in what here (though viciously and perversely) have I also imitated my Lord? Was it, that I had a desire to act against the Law by sleight where I could not by power; and, though restrained by it, yet would imitate a lame kind of liberty in doing, free from punishment, what I could not, free from guilt, out of a fond resemblance of thy Omnipotency?

# Dark waters
## William Whiting

*William Whiting (1825–78) spent the last 36 years of his life as master of the Quiristers of Winchester College. He published some volumes of poetry but his Hymn 'Eternal Father, strong to save' is far and away his most famous composition. It is usually sung to a tune by John Bacchus Dykes (1823–76), who also wrote music for 'Holy, holy, holy' by Reginald Heber and other hymns.*

O Holy Spirit, Who didst brood
Upon the waters dark and rude,

And bid their angry tumult cease,
And give, for wild confusion, peace;
O hear us when we cry to Thee
For those in peril on the sea.

5

# The legend of Christopher
# William Caxton

*Jacobus de Voragine (1230–98), who became Archbishop of Genoa, compiled*
The Golden Legend, *a collection of saints' stories of great influence. It was
one of the first books printed in England by William Caxton, in 1483, and it
is his translation that is given here. This is the classic version of the life of St
Christopher, who was widely honoured as a helper saint. His image was
painted in many British and continental churches, on the wall by the door,
where parishioners could see it on leaving. He is usually shown bearing his
palm-tree staff and fording the river with the Christ-child on his shoulder.
Although his intercession was sought as a real saint in heaven, his legend is a
tale of the search for a God-given vocation.*

Christopher was of the lineage of the Canaanites and he was of a
right great stature, and had a terrible and fearful cheer and
countenance. And he was twelve cubits of length, and as it is read
in some histories that, when he served and dwelt with the king of
Canaan, it came in his mind he would seek the greatest prince that
was in the world, and him would he serve and obey. And he came
to a right great king, whom the renome [renown] generally was
that he was greatest of the world. And when the king saw him he
received him into his service, and made him dwell in his court.
    Upon a time a minstrel sang tofore him a song in which he

named oft the devil. And the king, which was a Christian man, when he heard him name the devil, made anon sign of the cross in his visage. And when Christopher saw that, he had great marvel what sign it was, and wherefore the king made it, and he demanded of him. And because the king would not say, he said: 'If thou tell me not, I shall no longer dwell with thee.' And then the king told to him, saying: 'Alway when I hear the devil named, I fear that he should have power over me and I garnish me with this sign that he grieve nor annoy me.'

Then Christopher said to him: 'Doubtest thou the devil, that he hurt thee not? Then is the devil more mighty and greater than thou art. I am then deceived of my hope and purpose, for I had supposed I had found the most mighty and the most greatest Lord of the world. But I commend thee to God, for I will go seek him for to be my Lord, and I his servant.'

And then he hasted him for to seek the devil. And as he went by a great desert, he saw a great company of knights, of which a knight cruel and horrible came to him and demanded whither he went, and Christopher answered to him and said: 'I go seek the devil for to be my master.' And he said: 'I am he that thou seekest.' And then Christopher was glad, and bound him to be his servant perpetual, and took him for his master and Lord.

And as they went together by a common way, they found there a cross, erect and standing. And anon as the devil saw the cross he was afeard and fled, and left the right way, and brought Christopher about by a sharp desert. And after, when they were past the cross, he brought him to the highway that they had left. And when Christopher saw that, he marvelled, and demanded whereof he doubted, and had left the high and fair way, and had gone so far about by so aspre [harsh] a desert. And the devil would not tell him in no wise.

Then Christopher said to him: 'If thou wilt not tell me, I shall anon depart from thee, and shall serve thee no more.' Wherefore the devil was constrained to tell him, and said: 'There was a man called Christ which was hanged on the cross, and when I see his sign

I am sore afraid, and flee from it wheresoever I see it.' To whom Christopher said: 'Then he is greater, and more mightier than thou, when thou art afraid of his sign, and I see well that I have laboured in vain, when I have not founden the greatest Lord of the world. And I will serve thee no longer, go thy way then, for I will go seek Christ.'

And when he had long sought and demanded where he should find Christ, at last he came into a great desert, to an hermit that dwelt there, and this hermit preached to him of Jesus Christ and informed him in the faith diligently and said to him: 'This king whom thou desires to serve, requireth the service that thou must fast.' And Christopher said to him: 'Require me some other thing, and I shall do it, for that which thou requirest I may not do.' And the hermit said: 'Thou must then wake and make many prayers.' And Christopher said to him: 'I may do no such thing.' And then the hermit said to him: 'Knowest thou such a river, in which many be perished and lost?' To whom Christopher said: 'I know it well.' Then said the hermit: 'Because thou art noble and high of stature and strong in thy members, thou shalt be resident by that river, and thou shalt bear over all them that shall pass there, which shall be thing right convenable to our Lord Jesu Christ whom thou desirest to serve, and I hope he shall show himself to thee.' Then said Christopher: 'Certes, this service may I well do, and I promise to him for to do it.'

Then went Christopher to this river, and made there his habitacle for him and bare a great pole in his hand instead of a staff, by which he sustained him in the water, and bore over all manner of people without ceasing. And a time, as he slept in his lodge, he heard the voice of a child which called him and said: 'Christopher come out and bear me over.' Then he awoke and went out, but he found no man. And when was again in his house, he heard the same voice and he ran out and found nobody. The third time he was called and came thither, and found a child beside the rivage [bank] of the river, which prayed him goodly to bear him over the water.

And then Christopher lift up the child on his shoulders, and took his staff, and entered into the river for to pass. And the water of the river arose and swelled more and more: and the child was heavy as lead, and alway as he went farther the water increased and grew more, and the child more and more waxed heavy, insomuch that Christopher had great anguish and was afeard to be drowned. And when he was escaped with great pain, and passed the water, and set the child aground, he said to the child: 'Child, thou hast put me in great peril; thou weighest almost as I had all the world upon me, I might bear no greater burden.'

And the child answered: 'Christopher, marvel thee nothing, for thou hast not only borne all the world upon thee, but thou hast borne him that created and made all the world, upon thy shoulders. I am Jesu Christ the king, to whom thou servest in this work. And because that thou know that I say to be the truth, set thy staff in the earth by thy house, and thou shalt see to-morn that it shall bear flowers and fruit.'

And anon he vanished from his eyes. And then Christopher set his staff in the earth, and when he arose on the morn, he found his staff like a palmier bearing flowers, leaves and dates.

# 6

## Shrinking from duty
## Alfred the Great

*Alfred the Great (849–99) put in place a programme to make every Englishman literate. To this end, and in the cause of increasing the holiness of the clergy, he sent round to bishops copies of the* Pastoral Care *by Pope Gregory the Great which he himself translated laboriously with the help of his own clerical officials.*

*Gregory (540–604), as well as being respected as a learned doctor of the Western Church, was revered in England as the apostle of its conversion, for having sent Augustine of Canterbury from Rome in 596. In the* Pastoral Care *Gregory's theme is the qualities required of a bishop, or any Christian leader, and while he criticizes those who seek office out of worldly ambition, he also takes to task good and talented Christians who shrink from taking on responsibilities.*

Many are honoured with great gifts of many abilities and talents. They receive such gifts so they can teach many. For the sake of others they keep their bodies clean from sinful pleasures; they have the strength to be firm in abstinence; they are filled with the sweetmeats of learning; they are patient in troublesome things and in every weariness, and are humble in forbearance; they are active and bold in exercising virtue; they are courteous; they are austere and strict for righteousness' sake.

Those who are like this, and are asked to undertake a responsibility but refuse, often find that they lose the gifts that God has given them for the sake of other people, not for their own benefit alone. When they think exclusively how they themselves should become most perfect, and not how other people are getting on, they lose the very good that they desire exclusively themselves. Of such men Christ in his Gospel said: 'No man shall light a candle under a bushel.' And again he said to the apostle Peter: 'Peter, lovest thou me?' He said: 'Thou knowest that I love thee.' And then said the Lord: 'Feed my sheep, if thou lovest me.' If then the feeding of the sheep is a sign of love, why should anyone to whom God gives such abilities refuse to feed his flock, unless that he wishes to say that he does not love the Lord and the High Shepherd of all creatures?

Of such a person Paul the apostle said: 'If Christ died for all, then all men become dead. What is then better, while we live, than that we live not to the lusts of our flesh, but according to the commands of him who for us was dead and afterwards rose again?'

Of such a person Moses said: 'If anyone die and beget no child, if he leave a brother, let him take his wife to himself. If he then begets a child thereby, let him produce it for the brother that is dead, who once had her to himself. But if he will refuse his wife, then let her spit in his face, and let his relation take a shoe from his foot, that men may afterwards call his dwelling place the dwelling place of the unshod.' This was a righteous judgement under the old law; and it is parable to us now. The brother that died first stands for Christ. He showed himself after his resurrection and said: 'Go and tell my brethren to come to Galilee, there shall they see me.' He died as if he died without children, for he had not yet filled up the number of his chosen. So, as under the old law the living brother was bidden to take the dead brother's wife, so it is proper that the care of the Holy Church, which is the congregation of Christ's family, should be entrusted to him that has talents enough to serve it, and knows how to give good counsel to it. If therefore any one renounces it, then it is right for the wife to spit in his face, that is, that the congregation of the people should reprove him with the same force as if they spat in his face. Since he will neither give what God has given him, nor help the people with what God has helped him, it is right that the holy congregation should reprove everyone who desires good gifts to benefit himself alone and is unwilling to assist others. He shall rightly have one shoe removed, and people will call him, in reproach, the unshod one.

Of these, Christ said in his gospel: 'Shoe your feet, that you may be ready to go the way of peace, after the commandments of my books.' If then we have as much care and as great anxiety for our neighbours as for ourselves, we shall have both feet shod irreproachably. If, however, we disregard our neighbour's benefit, and concentrate on ours alone, one of our feet will be unshod, to our disgrace.

# Responsibilities of leadership
# Benedict of Nursia

*Benedict of Nursia (480–547) set up monasteries, notably Monte Cassino, and compiled the Rule which in simple, spare terms outlines the life of a monk. Western monasticism, with all the dissemination of culture it entailed, owed everything to him.*

*In his Rule, Benedict discusses how a Christian chosen to have care of others should seek to follow high standards, lest he bear the responsibility for the deterioration of those under him.*

An Abbot who is worthy to rule over the monastery ought always to remember what he is called, and correspond to his name of superior by his deeds. For he is believed to hold the place of Christ in the monastery, since he is called by His name, as the Apostle says: 'You have received the spirit of the adoption of children, in which we cry Abba, Father.' And therefore the Abbot ought not (God forbid) to teach, or ordain, or command anything contrary to the law of the Lord; but let his bidding and his doctrine be infused into the minds of his disciples like the leaven of divine justice.

Let the Abbot be ever mindful that at the dreadful judgement of God an account will have to be given both of his own teaching and of the obedience of his disciples. And let him know that to the fault of the shepherd shall be imputed any lack of profit which the father of the household may find in his sheep. Only then shall he be acquitted, if he shall have employed all pastoral diligence on his unruly and disobedient flock, and used all his care to amend their corrupt manner of life. Then shall he be absolved in the judgement of the Lord, and may say to the Lord with the prophet: 'I have not hidden thy justice in my heart, I have declared thy truth and thy salvation, but they contemned and despised me.' And then at length the punishment of death shall be inflicted on the disobedient sheep.

Therefore, when anyone receives the name of Abbot, he ought to govern his disciples by a two-fold teaching: that is, he should show goodness and holiness by his deeds rather than his words, declaring to the intelligent among his disciples the commandments of the Lord by words, but to the hard-hearted and the simple-minded setting forth the divine precepts by the example of his deeds. And let him show by his own actions that those things ought not to be done which he has taught his disciples to be against the law of God. Otherwise, while preaching to others, he might himself become a castaway, and God will say to him in his sin: 'Why do you declare my justice, and take my covenant in your mouth? You have hated discipline, and have cast my words behind thee.' And again, 'You who saw the mote in your brother's eye, did you not see the beam in your own?'

Let him make no distinction of persons in the monastery. Let not one be loved more than another, unless he be found to excel in good works or in obedience. Let not one of noble birth be put before one that was formerly a slave, unless some other reasonable cause exist for it. But if upon just consideration it should so seem good to the Abbot, let him arrange as he please concerning the place of anyone at all. Otherwise, let them keep their own places; because, whether bond or free, we are all one in Christ, and bear an equal rank in the service of one Lord: 'For with God there is no respecting of persons.' Only for one reason are we preferred in his sight, if we are found to outdo others in good works and in humility. Let the Abbot, then, show equal love to all, and let the same discipline be imposed upon all according to their deserts.

The Abbot in his teaching ought always to observe the bidding of the Apostle, where he says: 'Reprove, entreat, rebuke'. He should mingle, as occasions may require, gentleness with severity, showing now the rigour of a master, now the loving affection of a father, so as sternly to rebuke the undisciplined and restless, and to exhort the obedient, mild and patient to advance in virtue. And such as are negligent and haughty we charge him to reprove and correct. Let him not shut his eyes to the faults of offenders; but as soon as they appear, let him strive with all his might to root them out, remembering the fate of Heli, the priest of Silo. Those of good disposition and understanding let him, for the first and second time, correct only with words; but such as are froward and hard of heart, and proud, or disobedient, let him chastise with bodily stripes at the very first offence, knowing that it is written: 'The fool is not corrected with words.' And again: 'Strike your son with the rod, and thou shalt deliver his soul from death.'

The Abbot ought always to remember what he is, and what he is called, and to know that to whom more is committed, from him more is required; and he must consider how difficult and arduous a task he has undertaken, of ruling souls and adapting himself to many dispositions.

Let him so accommodate and suit himself to the character and intelligence of each, winning some by kindness, others by reproof, others by persuasion, that he may not only suffer no loss in the flock committed to him, but may even rejoice in their virtuous increase.

Above all, let him not, overlooking or undervaluing the salvation of the souls entrusted to him, care too much about passing, earthly and perishable things. But let him always bear in mind that he has undertaken the government of souls, and that he will have to give an account for them. He will not complain of the lack of worldly goods, if he remembers what is written: 'Seek first the kingdom of God and his justice, and all these things shall be added unto you.' And again: 'Nothing is wanting to them that fear him.'

And let him know that he who has undertaken the government of souls, must prepare himself to render an account of them. And whatever may be the number of the brethren under his care, let him be certainly assured that on the Day of Judgement he will have to give an account to the Lord of all these souls, as well as of his own.

And thus, being ever fearful of the coming inquiry which the Shepherd will make into the state of the flock committed to him, while he is careful on other men's account, he will be solicitous also on his own. And so, while correcting others by his admonitions, he will be himself cured of his own defects.

# PART 2

# Discovering God

# 8

## The still voice
## Thomas à Kempis

*Thomas à Kempis (1379–1471) entered the Augustinian monastery of Agnietenberg in 1400 and ended his life as its superior. His* Imitation of Christ, *written about 1420, met an appetite among lay people for books of devotion. It was translated into English during the author's lifetime (though published anonymously), and it has remained a favourite, against the odds, among English-speaking people ever since.*

*The translation here, from 1726, is by George Stanhope (1660–1728). Stanhope was Dean of Canterbury and published extracts from Augustine, Anselm and even the Jesuit Robert Parsons for a Protestant readership. When, in the nineteenth century, Henry Morley edited Stanhope's version of Thomas à Kempis for Sir John Lubbock's series of a hundred books, he wrote: 'The pithy style of the original is lost in flowing sentences that pleased the reader in Queen Anne's reign.'*

Speak, Lord for thy Servant heareth. Behold, I am thy Servant and the Son of thy Handmaid; O give me Understanding, that I may learn thy Commandments. Incline my Soul to the Words of thy Mouth, which drop down as the Rain upon the tender Herb, and drift gently, like Dew upon the Grass. The Israelites indeed besought Moses heretofore, 'Speak thou unto us, and we will hear, but let not God speak unto us, lest we die.' But let it not be done unto me, my God. I rather chuse to make my humble Petition in the Prophet Samuel's Form, 'Speak, Lord, for thy Servant heareth.' Let not Moses, nor any of the Prophets be my only Instructors, but do thou thy self also vouchsafe to teach me by thy self. For thou art the Source of all their Light and Knowledge. They could not utter Truth without thy Inspiration and Heavenly Guidance, but Thou art Essential Wisdom and Truth, and canst communicate thy self effectually to my Soul.

Their Words, alas, are Air and empty Sound, but Thine alone are Spirit and Life. Their Expressions may be proper, their Arguments moving, but unless thou break Silence, my Soul will still continue deaf and insensible. They deliver the Words, but thou art the Interpreter, and lettest me into the true and hidden Sense of their abstruse Oracles. Their Books are sealed and only thy Hand can open and explain them. From Them we receive the Command, but only from Thee the Disposition to Obey, and the whole Power of performing it. They shew the Way, but thou impartest the Strength to walk in it; all They can do, is still remote and without us. Thou only entrest into the Soul, and, by a secret Conveyance, putt'st Truth in the Inward Parts. 'Paul may plant, and Apollos water', but except thou be pleased 'to give the Increase, the Word will return unto thee void, and accomplish' no part of 'the End, whereto thou sentest it'. The Voice of their Cry pierces our Ears; but the knowing what they cry, and the Impression upon our Hearts, is thy peculiar Gift.

Therefore, I cannot but implore again thy Grace and Mercy, and beg, that Moses may not speak to me but thou, my Lord, my God, the Only and Eternal Truth, lest I die; Not by the Terrors of thy thund'ring Voice, but by the effectual Communications of thy Will. For if I be instructed and admonished by the Outward Ministration only, and be not inwardly disposed, and zealously affected to Obedience, the Advantages of Instruction will but aggravate my Condemnation. For this is the dismal Consequence of the Word 'preached not profiting, when it is not mixed with Faith in them that hear it'. And mixed with Faith thou knowest it cannot be, except seconded and enforced by the Voice of the Spirit; except thou incline me to love the Good I know, and enable me faithfully to fulfil the Doctrine I believe. 'Speak therefore, Lord', I say again; To thee thy Servant listens gladly, for 'Thou hast the Words of Eternal Life'. Speak powerfully to my Soul, and carry the Saving Truths home to my Conscience and Affections;

that thy Words may bring Comfort and Peace, Reformation and Holiness to thy attentive Servant, and to thy self immortal Honour and Praise.

# 9

# Thanksgiving for the body
# Thomas Traherne

*Thomas Traherne (1637–74), an Anglican clergyman, is like no other writer, although the systematic style of his* Thanksgivings *is reminiscent of both Lancelot Andrewes and Christopher Smart. He was noticed in his lifetime by the biographer Anthony Wood, but his reputation rested on the posthumous* Serious and Pathetical Contemplation of the Mercies of God *(1699), which contained the* Thanksgivings *from which the extract below comes. He was largely forgotten thereafter, being overlooked by the great nineteenth-century* Dictionary of National Biography.

*A remarkable series of accidents rescued his writings from obscurity: a manuscript containing his meditations called* Centuries *was found on a London book-barrow in 1896; in 1964 another manuscript of meditations was found; in 1967 another large manuscript was rescued from a burning rubbish dump in Lancashire.*

**Thanksgiving for the body**
   ... Blessed be thy holy Name,
     O Lord, my God!
  For ever blessed be thy holy Name,
     For that I am made
  The work of thy hands,
  Curiously wrought
     By thy divine Wisdom,

Enriched
  By thy Goodness,
Being more thine
  Than I am mine own.
O Lord!
  Thou hast given me a Body,
Wherein the glory of thy Power shineth,
Wonderfully composed above the Beasts,
Within distinguished into useful parts,
Beautified without with many Ornaments.
    Limbs rarely poised,
    And made for Heaven:
    Arteries filled
    With celestial Spirits:
    Veins, wherein Blood floweth,
    Refreshing all my Flesh,
      Like Rivers:
    Sinews fraught with the mystery
    Of wonderful Strength,
      Stability,
      Feeling.
O blessed be thy glorious Name!
That thou hast made it,
    A Treasury of Wonders,
    Fit for its several Ages;
    For Dissections,
    For Sculptures in Brass,
    For Draughts in Anatomy,
For the Contemplation of the Sages.
    Whose inward parts,
    Enshrined in thy Libraries,
      Are:
    The Amazement of the Learned,
    The Admiration of Kings and Queens,
    The Joy of Angels;

The Organs of my Soul,
The Wonder of Cherubims.
Those blinder parts of refined Earth,
Beneath my Skin;
Are full of thy Depths,
For many thousand Uses,
Hidden Operations,
Unsearchable Offices.
But for the diviner Treasures wherewith thou hast endowed
My Brains, Mine Eyes,
My Heart, Mine Ears,
My Tongue, My Hands,
O what Praises are due unto thee,
Who hast made me
A living Inhabitant
Of the great World.
And the Centre of it!
A sphere of Sense,
And a mine of Riches,
Which when Bodies are dissected fly away.
The spacious Room
Which thou hast hidden in mine Eye,
The Chambers for Sounds
Which thou hast prepar'd in mine Ear,
The Receptacles for Smells
Concealed in my Nose;
The feeling of my Hands,
The taste of my Tongue.
But above all, O Lord, the Glory of Speech, whereby thy
Servant is enabled with Praise to celebrate thee.
For
All the Beauties in Heaven and Earth,
The melody of Sounds,
The sweet Odours
Of thy Dwelling-place.

The delectable pleasures that gratifie my Sense,
That gratify the feeling of Mankind.
The Light of History,
Admitted by the Ear.
The Light of Heaven,
Brought in by the Eye.
The Volubility and Liberty
Of my Hands and Members.
Fitted by thee for all Operations;
Which the Fancy can imagine
Or Soul desire:
From the framing of a Needle's Eye,
To the building of a Tower:
From the squaring of Trees,
To the polishing of Kings' Crowns.
For all the Mysteries, Engines, Instruments, wherewith the
World is filled, which we are able to frame and use to
thy Glory.
For all the Trades, variety of Operations, Cities, Temples,
Streets, Bridges, Mariner's Compass, admirable Picture,
Sculpture, Writing, Printing, Songs and Musick,
wherewith the World is beautified and adorned.
Much more for the Regent Life,
And Power of Perception,
Which rules within.
That secret depth of fathomless Consideration
That receives the information
Of all our senses,
That makes our centre equal to the Heavens,
And comprehendeth in it self the magnitude of the World;
The involved mysteries
Of our common sense;
The inaccessible secret
Of perceptive fancy;
The repository and treasury

Of things that are past;
The presentation of things to come.
Thy Name be glorified
For evermore
For all the art which thou hast hidden
In this little piece
Of red clay.
For the workmanship of thy hand,
Who didst thy self form man
Of the dust of the ground,
And breath into his Nostrils
The breath of Life.
For the high Exaltation whereby thou hast glorified every body,
Especially mine,
As thou didst thy Servant
*Adam's* in *Eden.*
Thy Works themselves speaking to me the same thing that
was said unto him in the beginning,
WE ARE ALL THINE ...

# The lost nightingale
# Alcuin

*Alcuin (735–804) had been the Master of the Schools at York, building up the fine library there. In the 780s he was called to Aachen by Charlemagne to establish a school there. He spent the last eight years of his life at St Martin's Abbey, Tours, still teaching and writing, but occupied for the most part in tranquilly preparing for death. On the evidence of Alcuin's poetry, it is difficult to contemplate the fact that there were Dark Ages in Europe.*

*The translation here is that of Helen Waddell, from her* Mediaeval Latin Lyrics *(1929).*

**De luscinia**
Quae te dextra mihi rapuit, luscinia, ruscis,

63

illa meae fuerat invida laetitiae.
tu mea dulcisonis implesti pectora musis,
atque animum moestum carmine mellifluo.
qua propter veniant volucrum simul undique coetus,
carmine te mecum plangere Pierio.
spreta colore tamen fueras non spreta canendo.
lata sub angusto gutture vox sonuit,
dulce melos iterans vario modulamine Musae,
atque creatorem semper in ore canens.
noctibus in furvis nusquam cessavit ab odis,
vox veneranda sacris, o decus atque decor.
quid mirum, cherubim, seraphim si voce tonantem
perpetua laudent, dum tua sic potuit?

## Written for his lost nightingale

Whoever stole you from that bush of broom,
I think he envied me my happiness,
O little nightingale, for many a time
You lightened my sad heart from its distress,
And flooded my whole soul with melody.
And I would have the other birds all come,
And sing along with me thy threnody.

So brown and dim that little body was,
But none could scorn thy singing. In that throat,
That tiny throat, what depth of harmony,
And all night long ringing thy changing note.
What marvel if the cherubim in heaven
Continually do praise Him, when to thee,
O small and happy, such a grace was given?

# 10

# Perfection
# John Wesley

*John Wesley (1703–91) is known as the astonishingly energetic founder of Methodism (though he himself remained a lifelong cleric of the Church of England). While still at university, he and his circle sought a way of life that would facilitate holiness. Wesley spent the rest of his days striving for the same end. But what was holiness and what was the way? Many Methodists parted company with Wesley on the question of predestination, taking the Calvinist line.*

*The notes drawn up here show Wesley trying to formulate his thoughts in 1767 on the differences between justification and perfection and on the question of whether perfection left it possible for a person to sin.*

## Brief thoughts on Christian perfection

*London, 27 January 1767*
Some thoughts occurred to my mind this morning concerning Christian perfection, and the manner and time of receiving it, which I believe may be useful to set down.

1. By perfection I mean the humble, gentle, patient love of God, and our neighbour, ruling our tempers, words, and actions.

I do not include an impossibility of falling from it, either in part or in whole. Therefore, I retract several expressions in our Hymns, which partly express, partly imply, such an impossibility.

And I do not contend for the term sinless, though I do not object against it.

2. As to the manner. I believe this perfection is always wrought in the soul by a simple act of faith, consequently, in an instant.

But I believe a gradual work, both preceding and following that instant.

3. As to the time. I believe this instant generally is the instant of death, the moment before the soul leaves the body. But I believe it may be ten, 20, or 40 years before.

I believe it is usually many years after justification; but that it may be within five years or five months after it, I know no conclusive argument to the contrary.

If it must be many years after justification, I would be glad to know how many. *Pretium quotus arroget annus?*

And how many days or months, or even years, can any one allow to be between perfection and death? How far from justification must it be; and how near to death?

# Prayer at death
# Samuel Johnson

*Samuel Johnson (1709–84) had been suffering from dropsy, and was gasping for breath. He took opiates as a narcotic but could only sleep in a chair. He made his will, drew up epitaphs for his parents' and brother's memorial tablets in Lichfield church, burnt many private papers and sent his publisher a collection of prayers.*

*He had been troubled by scruples and fears of death, but his last prayer shows a calmness of mind. He died on 13 December 1784.*

*5 December 1784.* Almighty and most merciful Father, I am now, as to human eyes it seems, about to commemorate for the last time, the death of thy son Jesus Christ, our Saviour and Redeemer. Grant, O Lord, that my whole hope and confidence may be in his merits and in thy mercy: forgive and accept my late conversion, enforce and accept my imperfect repentance; make this commemoration of him available to the confirmation of my Faith, the establishment of my Hope, and the enlargement of my Charity, and make the Death of thy son Jesus effectual to my redemption. Have mercy upon me and pardon the multitude of my offences. Bless my Friends, have mercy upon all men. Support me by the Grace of thy Holy Spirit in the days of weakness, and at the hour of death, and receive me, at my death, to everlasting happiness, for the Sake of Jesus Christ. Amen.

# 11

## The appeal of the Blessed Virgin
## Oliver Bernard

*Oliver Bernard (born 1925) is a poet who has lived in Norfolk for 30 years. He has worked as an advisory teacher of drama and is a translator of the French poets Apollinaire and Rimbaud.*

Quia Amore Langueo, *a late fourteenth-century poem, exists in more than one fifteenth-century manuscript. Its second part was included in the* Oxford Book of English Verse, *but the 'Appeal of the Blessed Virgin Mary to Man' was hardly known until Oliver Bernard published a version in 1995, now republished in his* Verse &c. *(Anvil). His intention was to 'edge the texts just sufficiently out of Middle English to allow the complete poem the wide readership it undoubtedly merits'. The fourteenth-century spiritual writer Richard Rolle points out that the phrase* 'amore langueo' *occurs in the Song of Songs, 'and this is the English of those two words: "I languish for love"'.*

### Appeal of the Blessed Virgin Mary to man
>        In an alcove of a tower,
>        As I stood musing on the moon,
>        A crowned queen of great honour
>        I saw in a spiritual vision;

And she lamented there alone,
For human souls were wrapped in woe,
'I cannot leave mankind alone,
  *Quia amore langueo.*

I long for love of man my brother,
I plead for pardon of his vice,
I am his mother – I can no other –
Why should I my dear child despise?
Though he provoke me in diverse wise
And through his frailty fall, even so
We must pity him until he rise,
  *Quia amore langueo.*

I bide, I bide in great longing,
I watch till men my love will crave;
I complain for pity of their pining;
Should they beg mercy, they would it have,
Sue to me, soul, and I shall save;
Bid me, my child, and I shall go;
You prayed me never but my Son forgave,
  *Quia amore langueo.*

O wretch in the world, I look on thee,
I see thy trespass day by day,
With lechery against my chastity,
With pride against my poor array.
My love is constant, thine is away;
My love thee calls, thou stealest me fro;
Turn to me, sinner, I thee pray,
  *Quia amore langueo,*

Mother of mercy I was for thee made;
Who needeth it now but thou alone?
To get thee grace I am more glad

Than thou to ask it: why wilt thou none?
When said I Nay to any one?
Forsooth never yet, to friend nor foe;
When thou askest not, then I make moan,
    *Quia amore langueo.*

I seek thee in weal and wretchedness,
I seek thee in riches and poverty;
Thou man behold where thy mother is:
Why lovest thou me not, since I love thee?
However sinful or sorry thou be,
More welcome to me there is no one more;
I am thy sister, trust thou in me,
    *Quia amore langueo.*

My child is condemned for thy sin,
My bairn is beaten for thy trespass;
It pricks my heart that thou my near kin
Shouldst be dis-eased or damned, alas!
O Jesu, his brother, thy mother I was;
Thou suckedst my pap, thou lovest man so,
Thou died for him; my heart he has,
    *Quia amore langueo.*

Man, leave thy sin, then, for my sake;
Why should I give thee that thou not would?
And yet if thou sin, some prayer take,
And trust in me as I have told.
Am I not thy mother called?
Why should I leave thee? I love thee so;
I am thy friend, I help thee, behold,
    *Quia amore langueo.*

When I say Yea wilt thou say Nay?
I have power to help thee to bliss;

Heartily if thou to me pray,
I shall forgive thy deeds amiss.
O sinful man, I tell thee this:
The hundredth year thou wert me fro
I should thee welcome, clip and kiss,
　　*Quia amore langueo.*

I am mankind's help, acknowledging;
When they will call, I shall restore;
I love to save my own offspring.
Now will I tell of this matter more:
No wonder my heart to Jesu cling;
I am his mother, what else can I do?
For his sake have I this worshipping,
　　*Quia amore langueo.*

Why was I crowned and made a queen?
Why was I called of mercy the well?
Why should an earthly woman have been
Placed high in heaven, above angel?
For thee, mankind; it is truth I tell;
Ask me for help and I shall do
What I was ordained for: keep thee from hell,
　　*Quia amore langueo.*

Now, man, have mind on me for ever;
Look on thy love thus languishing!
Let us never from each other dissever;
My help is thine own; creep under my wing.
Thy sister's a queen, thy brother a king,
Inheritance sure! Son, come thereunto:
Join hands with me, and learn thou to sing:
　　"*Quia amore langueo*".'

# Tied to God
# Henry Vaughan

*Henry Vaughan (1622–93) appended 'Silurist' to his name, which meant no more than that he lived in Brecknockshire, in the Usk valley. He was a cousin of John Aubrey, sharing his antiquarian disposition, a royalist, a physician, a layman, unlike his twin brother Thomas, who was a clergyman. His volume of religious poetry,* Silex Scintillans, *made little mark in his own time, but was greatly admired from the nineteenth century onward, the poem 'They are all gone into the world of light' remaining a favourite.*

## The knot

Bright Queen of Heaven! God's Virgin Spouse,
   The glad world's blessed maid!
Who beauty tyed life to thy house,
   And brought us saving ayd.

Thou art the true Love's-knot; by thee
   God is made our Allie,
And man's inferior Essence he
   With his did dignifie.

For Coalescent by that Band
   We are his body grown,
Nourished with favours from his hand
   Whom for our head we own.

And such a Knot, what arm dares loose
   What life, what death can sever?
Which us in him, and him in us
   United keeps for ever.

# 12

# The love of Jesus
# Richard Rolle

*Richard Rolle (1290–1349) was one of the half-dozen English writers of the fourteenth century widely prized for their description of the life of prayer. He wrote in Latin and in English for those dedicated to a cloistered religious life, and lay people also benefited from the hundreds of manuscripts of his work that circulated. Many went unprinted for hundreds of years. The passage here, from* The Form of Perfect Living, *remained in manuscript until Clare Kirchberger transcribed it in the 1950s for her anthology* The Coasts of the Country. *The translation she made was obscure, so I have adapted it.*

Singular love is when all comfort and solace is excluded from the heart, except that but of Jesus alone. It desires no other delight or other joy. For in this condition his sweetness is so comforting and so lasting, his love so burning and gladdening, that he or she who is in this condition feels the fire of love burning in their soul, just as you might feel your finger burn if you put it into the fire. But that other fire to which I refer, if it is hot, is so delightful and wonderful that it is beyond my telling.

Then the soul is loving Jesus, thinking of Jesus, desiring Jesus, depending only on wanting him. sighing for him, burning for him, resting in him. Then comes the song of loving and of love. Then your thoughts turn to song and melody. Then it is right for you to sing the psalms that before you said. Then you must spend long in reciting a few psalms. Then you will think your death sweeter than honey, for then you will be most sure of seeing him whom you love. Then you will hardly be able to say: 'I languish for love', for then you will be able to say: 'I sleep and my heart wakes.'

If you want to remain with God and want grace to rule your life and want to come to the joy of love, fasten this name of Jesus so firmly in your heart that it can never slip out of your thoughts. And when you speak to him and by habit say 'Jesus', it will be joy in your ear, and honey in your mouth, and music in your heart. For you shall feel joy in hearing that name named, sweetness in speaking it, gladness and song in thinking it. If you think of Jesus continually and make that a constant state of mind, that will purge your sin and kindle your heart. It will clarify your soul. It will remove anger and chase away sloth. It will wound you with love, fill you with charity. It will repel the devil and remove fear. It will open heaven and make you a contemplative.

Keep Jesus in mind, for that removes all vices and imaginings from the lover. And hail Mary often, by day and by night.

You will have great love and feel much joy if you follow this advice. You will not have much want for books: keep love in your heart and in your work and you shall have everything we say or write of. The fulness of the law is charity; on that everything depends.

# Abandonment to Jesus
# Henry VI

*Henry VI (1421–71), whatever his political fortunes, was in his own time and after his death reputed as a saint. He founded the College of Our Lady of Eton and the College of Our Lady and St Nicholas (King's College) Cambridge. Henry VII set about building what is now Henry VII's chapel at Westminster Abbey to house his remains.*

**A prayer**
O Lord Jesus Christ, who didst create me, redeem me, and foreordain me unto that which I now am: Thou knowest what Thou wilt do with me: deal with me according to thy will and thy mercy.

73

# 13

## Rex Gentium
## Pacificus Baker

*Pacificus Baker (1695–1774) was a Franciscan friar who wrote six or seven manuals of devotion for fellow religious and for pious lay people. They were praised, in the days when such words were not yet pejorative, for having 'unction, solidity and moderation'. The passage below comes from his book,* The Christian Advent, *published in London in 1755. It takes the gospels for Sundays, Wednesdays and Fridays in Advent (Wednesday and Friday being in those days devoted to particular prayer and self-denial in Lent or Advent) and provides brief reflections and a series of pious exclamations intended to aid private prayer. It also gives the same treatment for the seven 'Great O's' – the antiphons for the seven days before Christmas. The one given here is for 21 December.*

**O Rex Gentium et desideratus earum, Lapisque angularis, qui facis utraque unum: veni et salva hominem quem de Limo formasti.**

**(O King of the Gentiles and their desired one, and the Corner Stone who maketh both one: Come and save Man whom thou hast form'd out of the Slime of the Earth.)**
As with God there is no Exception of Persons, and as the Son of God came into the World to save all Mankind; to break down the Partition Wall between Jew and Gentile; he is in this Antiphon called the Corner-Stone of that spiritual Building, his Church consisting of all who truly believe in him. For as he created all and every one, Salvation in his Name is preached and offer'd to every one. This universal Mercy and Goodness we are now to confess, and with grateful Hearts, and the warmest Sentiments of Acknowledgement, adore Jesus the Son of God born of the Blessed Virgin

and now coming into the World that the World might be sav'd by him; that Man form'd out of the Dust of the Earth might be translated from Earth to the Glory and never ending Happiness of Heaven.

## Devout Aspirations on this Antiphon

O my God and my Lord! O Jesus Redeemer of Mankind! Thou art truly King of the Gentiles, and of all the Nations of the Earth. Thou art the desired One, in whom all Nations shall put their Trust, and all Corners of the Earth be blessed. Thou art the Corner-Stone who maketh both one. Thou hast broken down the Partition wall between Jew and Gentile, and of both hast made one chosen Nation, a holy People, a Royal Priesthood. Thou art that Corner-Stone which the foolish Builders did reject, but art nevertheless become the Head Stone of the Corner. By thee, O Lord, was this done, and it is marvellous in our Eyes. Thy Favours, O Lord, are no longer confined to one peculiar People. Thou hast diffus'd the Sweetness of thy Mercy round all the Earth. All Nations have seen the Salvation sent by God. This was the Effect of thy Goodness, in order to save Man whom thou hadst made out of the Slime of the Earth.

Thou didst make Man after thine own Image and Likeness, O thou bountiful Creator of all Things that are made! Thou dids't create him pure, innocent and upright, and didst design him to be eternally happy with thee; but alas! he soon left his Innocence and forfeited that Happiness by Sin, which justly condemn'd him to all the Miseries of this life, and depriv'd him of the Happiness of the next. In this sad condition thou didst take pity on him, and wouldst thyself become his Redeemer. My God! How great is thy Love to Man! How hast thou defeated the Devil's Malice, and turn'd that to his greater Confusion wherein he gloried! He gloried in the Ruin of Man, in having drawn him into Rebellion against thee, and from thence thou didst show thy Power and thy Love, in vouching to redeem Man from the sad State he was in, to pardon his Crime, and to restore him to thy Favour again.

This Mercy thou didst promise to Man soon after his Fall, and to fulfil thy Promise didst first send thy Prophets to declare thy Coming, and to prepare the World to receive thee. Then in the Fulness of thine own Time didst thou descend from Heaven into the Pure Womb of a Chaste Virgin, and by joining our human Nature to thy divine Nature, like a select Corner-Stone didst become a Man-God, a God-Man, that thereby thou mightest save Man. Thus didst thou come, O desired of all Nations! Thus didst thou come full of Grace and Truth. O my God, how true and faithful art thou to thy Promise! Then, when the World deserv'd it least, when all Flesh was corrupted, then did the Truth of thy Promises appear. Then didst thou come, O King of the Gentiles! Accompanied with all the Graces of Heaven; and lest I should be afraid and terrified at thy Grandeur, thou comest clothed with my Weakness and Misery, that I might not fear to approach thee. O Jesus the Saviour of my Soul! I adore thee, and how ought I to love thee, who art thus come to save and free me from the Miseries of this World!

This was thy first Coming, when thou didst appear in great Poverty and Weakness, a tender weeping Infant subject to all the Infirmities of our human Nature, and wherein we behold thee truly Man. Thou wilt come again in great Power and Majesty, and wherein we shall see thee truly God; and in this respect thou art also the desired of all Nations, the Desire of thy faithful Servants who sigh after and wish for thy Coming in Glory. Then wilt thou put the last and finishing stroke to the Designs of thy Goodness, by rewarding those who love and serve thee. Hasten this thy Coming, O Lord! Call all Nations to the Knowledge of thee. Hasten to accomplish the Number of thy Elect, and call us all home to the Enjoyment of thee. O come and deliver us from this Land of Misery and Exile, and conduct us to that Happiness thou hast prepared for us. Remember that we are the Work of thy Hands, and thou didst make us of the Slime of the Earth. Thou didst make us, O Lord, for thyself, and to enjoy thee. O take us to thyself, that we may be happy with thee! This is what my soul earnestly desires, and for this will I wait with Patience and Resignation to thy good Pleasure, and sweeten the Bitterness of Delay with the comfortable Hopes of seeing and enjoying thee in thine own good Time.

# All our riches
# Francis of Assisi

*Francis of Assisi (1182–1226) wrote these praises of God one Lent, two years before his death, for Brother Leo, one of the first of his companions. They are preserved in a manuscript in Francis' own hand at the basilica at Assisi; it is hard to read, for Brother Leo kept it with him, folded up. He attributed to it the good resolution of some temptations he had been troubled by.*

## Praises of God

You are holy, Lord, the only God,
and your deeds are wonderful.
You are strong.
You are great.
You are the Most High,
You are almighty.
You, holy Father, are
King of heaven and earth.
You are Three and One,
Lord God, all good.
You are Good, all Good, supreme Good,
Lord God, living and true.
You are love,
You are wisdom.
You are humility,
You are endurance.
You are rest,
You are peace.
You are joy and gladness.
You are justice and moderation.
You are all our riches,

And you suffice for us.
You are beauty.
You are gentleness.
You are our protector,
You are our guardian and defender.
You are courage.
You are our haven and our hope.
You are our faith,
Our great consolation.
You are our eternal life,
Great and wonderful Lord,
God almighty,
Merciful Saviour.


# 14

# Jesus born in us
## Bernard of Clairvaux

*Bernard of Clairvaux (1090–1153) was at the heart of the greatest reform of monasticism that the West has seen. The monks of the Cistercian family, taking their name from the mother house at Cîteaux, looked for a simpler way of life than that of the dominant (Benedictine) tradition at the time. Bernard did not instigate the reform but gave his tremendous energies to it. Though he was always in bad health, there was a gentle, humane side to Bernard. He had particular devotion to the Child Jesus and wrote repeatedly on the Nativity. The passage below is from one of the meditations that he led for his monastic brothers, and it follows the medieval method of symbolism and typology.*

Would to God that we might be as Bethlehem in Judea, and that Jesus would deign to be born in us also; and that we might be worthy to hear said to us: 'To you that fear My Name shall the Sun of Righteousness arise with healing in His wings'(Malachi 4.2). For perhaps these words which we have cited above signify that there is need to sanctify ourselves and to be ready in order to see the glory of the Lord in us. For, according to the Prophet, 'Judah became his sanctification' (Psalm 113.2 [in the Vulgate translation]), which implies that by confession of sins all are purified. As to the word Bethlehem, which signifies 'House of Bread', it seems to me to have the meaning of *preparation*. For in what respect is a person prepared to receive so great a guest, who says: 'In my house there is no bread' (Isaiah 3.7)? It was because he was thus unprepared, that a certain man in the Gospel was obliged to go in the middle of the night to knock at the door of a friend, and say, 'A friend of mine is come to me in his journey and I have nothing to set before him' (Luke 11.6).

It is no doubt of the righteous man that the prophet says: 'His heart is fixed, trusting in the Lord. His heart is established, he shall not be afraid' (Psalm 112.7). There is no heart prepared which is not established. Now we know from the testimony of the same prophet that 'it is bread which strengtheneth man's heart' (Psalm 104.15). The heart of him, therefore, who is forgetful to eat his bread, is not prepared, but is bloodless and dry, while on the contrary, he who is forgetful of the things which are behind and presses forward unto those which are before, that he may keep the commandments which give life, is prepared and is not troubled. You see that there are certain things to be avoided, and certain things of which forgetfulness is to be desired. It was not the entire tribe of Manasseh which passed the Jordan, nor the whole which obtained for itself settlement on this side of the river (Joshua 13). There are those who are forgetful of God their Creator, and there are those who keep Him ever before their eyes, who are forgetful of their own people and their father's house. The former forget heavenly things; the latter, earthly: the one the present, the other the future; the one forgets the things which are seen, the other those which are of Jesus Christ. They are as the two half tribes of

Manasseh, and each is forgetful; but the one forgets Jerusalem, the other Babylon: the one forgets those things which are calculated to hinder him in his onward course, and he is therefore prepared; the other, on the contrary, forgets more the things which would be of profit to him than those which would not; and therefore is entirely unprepared to behold the glory of the Lord in himself.

This is not that 'House of Bread' in which the Saviour is born; nor this that of Manasseh to whom He appears, who is the Ruler of Israel, who sitteth between the Cherubim, according to the words of the Psalmist: 'Before Ephraim, Benjamin and Manasses, stir up Thy strength' (Psalm 80.2). I suppose that these three tribes represent those who are saved, whom another prophet has named 'Noah, Daniel and Job' (Ezekiel 14.14): and who are also recalled by those three shepherds to whom at the birth of the Messenger of the great Covenant, an Angel announced good tidings of great joy.

The three Magi also perhaps are types of those who come not from the East only, but also from the West, to sit down with Abraham, Isaac and Jacob. It seems perhaps that to Ephraim (which word signifies Fruitfulness) it belonged not unfitly to offer incense: for to offer incense, an offering of sweet savour, is the proper duty of those whom the Lord has set to go and to bring forth fruit, that is, to the rulers of the Church. As for Benjamin (son of the right hand), he necessarily offers gold, that is, the substance of this world: just as the faithful people who are placed at the right hand of the Judge, merit to he told by Him: 'I was an hungred and ye gave Me meat', etc. (Matthew 25.35). Furthermore, Manasseh, if he has desired that it should be he to whom God should appear, would offer the myrrh of mortification, which I consider to be especially required from those of our profession. And these remarks are made so that we may belong not to that part of the tribe of Manasseh which remained on the east side of Jordan, but that we may forget those things which are behind, and press forward to those which are before.

Now let us return to Bethlehem, and see what has taken place there; which the Lord has done and has revealed unto us. It is the 'House of Bread', as we have said: therefore it is good for us to be there. For where the Word of God is, there is not wanting that bread which strengthens the heart, as says the prophet: 'Strengthen Thou me with Thy Words' (Psalm 119.28). Without doubt, man lives by every word which proceedeth out of the mouth of God: he lives in Christ and Christ in him. There is He born, there He manifests Himself: He loves not the heart that is inconstant and vacillating, but that which is firm and stable. If anyone murmurs, hesitates, wavers, meditates returning to his vomit and being again wallowing in the mire, renouncing his vow and changing his purpose of life, he is not that Bethlehem, the House of Bread, in which Christ is born. For famine only, famine the most severe, obliges him to descend into Egypt, to feed the swine, to live upon husks, because he is dwelling far from the House of Bread, the house of the Father: in which, as is well known, even the hired servants have bread enough and to spare. Christ is not born in the heart of such an one to which is wanting a warm faith, which is the very bread of life, according to the statement of Scripture, 'The just shall live by faith' (Habakkuk 2.4), that is to say, the true life of the soul (which is Jesus Himself) does not, at the present, dwell in our hearts except by faith.

How can Jesus be born in him, how can salvation arise for him, when the true and perfectly certain declaration is 'Whosoever endureth to the end, shall be saved' (Matthew 10.22)? Plainly, Christ will not be found in him, nor will he be of those of whom it is said, 'ye leave an unction from the Holy One' (I John 2.20); from which it plainly appears, that his heart is doubtless dried up and withered, from the moment that he has forgotten to eat of this his bread. Much less does one who is of this character, belong to the Son of God, who is such, that His Spirit rests only upon the soul which is peaceful and humble and which trembles at His word (Isaiah 66.2); nor can there be any fellowship between unchanging eternity and such inconstancy; between Him who is the same for ever and one who never remains in the same state. But, furthermore, however firm we are and strong in the faith, however well prepared, however abounding in the bread of life which He

81

bestows upon us liberally, to Whom we say daily in our prayers, 'Give us this day our daily bread', we need always to add to our prayers, 'Forgive us our trespasses' (Matthew 6.11). For if we say that we have no sin we deceive ourselves and the truth is not in us (I John 1.8). Now the Truth is He who is born not simply in Bethlehem, but in Bethlehem of Judea, Jesus Christ, the Son of God.

## Star of the sea

*This liturgical hymn dates back to at least the ninth century. It was used at Vespers for feasts of the Virgin Mary, and was set to music by Josquin de Prez and Monteverdi among others.*

> Ave maris stella,
> Dei Mater alma,
> atque semper Virgo,
> felix caeli porta.
> Sumens illud Ave
> Gabrielis ore,
> funda nos in pace,
> mutans Hevae nomen.

[Hail, Star of the Sea, God's own Mother, ever Virgin, happy gate of heaven. Set us in peace, you who have changed Eve's name by taking that *Ave* which Gabriel spoke.]

> Solve vincula reis,
> profer lumen caecis
> mala nostra pelle,
> bona cuncta posce.
> Monstra te esse matrem:
> sumat per te preces,
> qui pro nobis natus,
> tulit esse tuus.

[Break the fetters of sin, give light to the blind, chase evil from us, pray for all blessings. Show thyself a Mother, and may He who was born for us through you hear our prayers through you.]

> Virgo singularis,
> inter omnes mites,
> nos culpis solutos,
> mites fac et castos.
> Vitam praesta puram,
> iter para tuum:
> ut videntes Iesum
> semper collaetemur.

[Virgin most excellent, mildest amongst women, free us from fault and make us chaste and mild. Keep our life pure and make our way safe, till in seeing Jesus we rejoice together for ever.]

# 15

# God with us
# Lady Lucy Herbert

*Lady Lucy Herbert (1669–1744) was the fifth and youngest daughter of the first marquess of Powis and his wife Elizabeth, the daughter of the second marquess of Worcester. She left everything at the age of twenty-four to join the convent of the Augustinian Canonesses at Bruges, where she became prioress in 1709.*

*Her* Several Excellent Methods of Hearing Mass *was published in 1722. Sometimes rather arbitrarily it connects actions of the liturgy to events in the life of Jesus, a technique that develops the devotional writings of Durandus (1237–96) Here she focuses on the identification of Jesus present in the Eucharist with Jesus who was born in Bethlehem, and she then considers conformity to the will of God.*

## A Manner of hearing Mass in Honour of the Incarnation and Nativity of our Saviour; to be used on the 25th of each Month, that being the Day of the Month that Jesus Christ was incarnate, and born for Love of us

*At the Beginning of the Mass*
When the priest descends the steps of the Altar, reflect how the world had been irrecoverably lost, if the word of God had not been pleased to descend from heaven into the womb of the blessed Virgin, and become man to redeem us from eternal Misery.

Render thanks to the most blessed Trinity, for being pleased to make use of so admirable a means to work our Salvation. Thank God the Father for loving the world so much as to give his only Son for it. Thank God the Son for abasing himself so far, as to cloath himself with our flesh and subject himself to our miseries. Thank God the Holy Ghost for operating this so admirable a mystery; and for forming of the blessed Virgin's purest blood the body of Christ, which afterwards was to be nailed for us upon a Cross.

*At the Gloria in Excelsis*
Reflect how all the Angels in heaven celebrated a feast at the moment the word was incarnate; rejoicing that by that means men would fill up the vacant places caused by the fall of Lucifer and his followers. What ought to be our joy who have so great an interest in it!

But this advantage, we must understand, regards only persons of good-will; that is, of a will conformable to God's will, docile to his voice, and who faithfully practise his law. Endeavour to be of that number.

*At the Offertory*
Consider how Jesus Christ, from the first moment of his conception, cloathed with human nature, as with sacerdotal vestments, begins

his Sacrifice. My God, said he, you would have no more oblations nor victims, but you have formed me a body. Holocaust and Sacrifices are no more agreeable to you for sin; then, said I, behold I come, as it stands written at the beginning of the book. I come, my God to do your will.

Since Jesus Christ is willing to be immolated for your sins, conceive a firm hope to obtain remission of them; beg him to offer himself again for those you have lately committed, that you may obtain pardon for them, and the grace of a sincere repentance and contrition.

Grieve that it was not in your power to consecrate yourself to Almighty God from the first moment that your soul animated your body. At least, offer yourself now to Jesus Christ, united to him as a member of his mystical body; and resolve to sacrifice the remainder of your life to the accomplishment of his divine will.

*At the Canon of the Mass*
Call to mind the longing desires of the Patriarchs and Prophets, to see the Messiah, and the continual sighs sent up to heaven to beg him to hasten his coming. Join yours to theirs, and press our Saviour to descend upon the Altar, saying with those holy souls, O heaven, grant us the just man we expect; he will be to us as a refreshing dew, and will render our souls fruitful of all good works.

*At the Consecration*
At the very moment that the Priest pronounces the words of Consecration, imagine how the Angels in great numbers descend with their Lord King: We announce to you great joy, for this day your Saviour is born for you.

Acknowledge him and adore him under the appearance of bread and wine. It is the same God whom the blessed Virgin held in her arms, wrapt in swaddling clouts and laid in a manger.

*At the Division of the Host*
When the Priest parts the Host, call to mind the painful

85

Circumcision of our Saviour. See how at the same moment that he takes the name of Jesus, he does the office, shedding his blood for our salvation. Desire ardently to receive that Sacred Blood into your heart, one drop of it is capable to sanctify the whole world. Reflect what may be the reason why, after having so often received it, you remain still the same.

*At the Agnus Dei*
Reflect that it is not without mystery that Jesus Christ is born in a stable, which is to signify that, there is no heart, however poor and vile it be, which he disdains to enter, provided it desires his coming, and disposes itself for the same. Secondly, reflect that he is the Lamb of God who was sacrificed on the Cross for our sins, and is desirous, on the Altar of our heart, to offer himself again to his Eternal Father for the same end.

Prepare yourself for this Divine Victim, that your soul may be fed with the Body and Blood of the Innocent Lamb.

*At the End of Mass*
After having received him really or spiritually, entertain your Divine Saviour, and beg him to remain hidden in your heart as he was at Nazareth, that so he may help you to labour and work as he did his blessed parents; and work with you joining his hand to yours, without which, acknowledge that nothing will be done well.

Resolve, as much as he shall by his grace enable you, to be watchful, and careful to secure him from the persecutions which daily and hourly will be raised against him, attempting at his life: For sin, as well as Herod, seeks to destroy him. See how you may defend him, and arm yourself against that monster.

# 16

# Recognizing Jesus
# Robert Southwell

*Robert Southwell (1561–95) wrote* Mary Magdalen's Tears *while staying at Arundel House in the Strand in London while he was engaged in pastoral work as a priest in disguise. The penal laws declared the presence of a Catholic priest in England treasonable. Southwell combined the Elizabethan accomplishments of courage and poetry with a deep religious idealism. He was arrested the next year, severely tortured and imprisoned until 1595, when he was tried, found guilty and hanged.*

Mary Magdalen's Tears *circulated in manuscript and was actually printed by an ordinary bookseller while Southwell was still alive. It is an imaginative meditation, very much of its time, on the risen humanity of Jesus and his recognition by one who loved him.*

**Jesus saith unto her, 'Marie'; shee turning, saith unto him, 'Rabboni'.**
O loving Master, thou diddest only deferre her consolation, to increase it, that the delight of thy presence might be so much the more welcome, in that through thy long absence it was with so little hope so much desired.

Thou wert content shee should lay out for thee so many sighs, teares, and plaints, and diddest purposely adjourne the date of her payment, to requite the length of these delays with a larger loan of joy. It may be shee knew not her former happinesse, till shee was weaned from it: nor had a right estimate in valuing the treasures with which thy presence did enrich her, untill her extreme poverty taught her their unestimable rate. But now thou shewest by a sweet experience, that though shee payd thee with the dearest water of her eyes, with her best breath, and tenderest love, yet small was the price that shee bestowed in respect of the worth shee received. Shee sought thee dead, and imprisoned in a stony jayle, and now shee findeth thee both alive, and at full liberty. Shee sought thee shrined in a shroud, more like a leper than thyselfe, left as the modell of the uttermost misery, and the only paterne of the bitterest unhappinesse; and now shee findeth thee invested in the robes of glory, the president of the highest, and both the owner and giver of all felicity.

And as all this while she hath sought without finding, wept without comfort, and called without answers: so now thou diddest satisfie her seeking with thy comming, her teares with thy triumph, and all her cryes with this one word, *Mary.*

For when shee heard thee call her in thy wonted manner, and with thy usuall voyce, her only name issuing from thy mouth wrought so strange an alteration in her, as if shee had beene wholly new made, when shee was only named. For whereas before the violence of her griefe had so benummed her, that her body seemed but the hearse of her dead heart, and the coffin of an unliving soule, and her whole presence but a representation of a double funerall, of thine and of her owne: now with this one word her senses are restored, her minde lightned, her heart quickened, and her soule revived.

But what marvell though with one word hee raise the dead spirits of his poore disciple, that with a word made the world, and even in this very word sheweth an omnipotent power?

*Marie* shee was called, as well in her bad as in her reformed estate, and both her good and evill was all of Marie's working. And as Marie signifieth no lesse what shee was, than what shee is; so is this one word, by his vertue that speaketh it, a repetition of all her miseries, an epitome of his mercies, and a memoriall of all her better fortunes. And therefore it laid so generall a discovery of herselfe before her eyes, that it awaked her most forgotten sorrowes, and mustered together the whole multitude of her joyes, and would have left the issue of their mutiny very doubtfull but that the presence and notice of her highest happinesse decided the quarrell, and gave her joyest the victory.

For as hee was her only Sunne, whose going downe left nothing but a dumpish night of fearefull fancies, wherein no starre of hope shined, and the brightest planets were changed into dismall signes: so the serenity of his countenance, and authority of his word, brought a calme and well-tempered day, that chasing away all darknesse, and dispersing the clouds of melancholy, cured the lethargy and brake the dead sleepe of her astonied [astonished] senses.

She therefore, ravished with his voyce, and impatient of delayes; taketh his talke out of his mouth, and to his first and yet only word answered but one other, calling him *Rabboni*, that is, master. And then sudden joy rowsing all other passions, shee could no more proceed in her owne than give him leave to goe forward with his speech.

Love would have spoken, but fears inforced silence. Hope frameth the words, but doubt melteth them in the passage: and when her in-ward conceits served to come out, her voice trembled, her tongue faltered, her breath failed. In fine, teares issued in lieu of words, and deepe sighs instead of long sentences, the eyes supplying the tongue's default, and the heart pressing out the unsyllabled breath at once, which the conflict of her disagreeing passions would not suffer to be sorted into the severall sounds of intelligible speeches.

For such is their estate that are sicke with a surfet of sudden joy, for the attaining of a thing vehemently desired. For as desire is ever ushered by hope, and waited on by feare, so is it credulous in entertaining conjectures, but hard in grounding a firme beleefe. And though it be apt to admit the least shadow of wished comfort; yet the hotter the desire is to have it, the more perfect assurance it requireth for it which no long as it wanteth the first newes or apparence of that which is in request, is rather an alarum to summon up all passions, than retreit to quiet the desire. For as hope presumeth the best, and inviteth joy to gratulate the good successe; so feare suspecteth it too good to be true, and calleth up sorrow to bewaile the uncertainty. And while these enterchange objections and answers, sometimes feare falleth into despaire, and hope riseth into repining anger; and thus the skirmish still continueth, till evidence of proofe conclude the controversie.

Marie therefore though shee suddenly answered upon notice of his voyce, yet because the novelty was so strange, his person so changed, his presence so unexpected, and so many miracles laid at once before her amazed eyes, shee found a sedition in her thoughts, till more earnest viewing him exempted them from all doubt.

And then, though words would have broken out, and her heart sent into his duties that shee ought him, yea, every thought striving to be first uttered, and to have the first roome in his gracious hearing, shee was forced as an indifferent arbiter among them, to seale them up all under silence by suppressing speech, and to supply the want of words, with more significant actions. And therefore running to the haunt of her chiefest delights, and falling at his sacred feet, shee offered to bathe them with teares of joy, and to sanctifie her lips, with kissing his once grievous, but now most glorious wounds.

Shee stayed not for any more words, being now made blessed with the Word himselfe, thinking it a greater benefit at once to feed all her wishes, in the homage, honour, and embracing of his feet, than in the often hearing of his lesse comfortable talke.


## 17

# The life and the death
# Ronald Knox

*Ronald Knox (1888–1957) was known for his wit and powers of parody even after his ordination as a priest, when he continued to support himself by writing. One of four remarkable sons of the Bishop of Manchester, he became a Catholic, was ordained and undertook the great work of making a new translation of the Bible, which he completed in 1955. He also produced the scholarly history* Enthusiasm, *together with a string of devotional, apologetic and satirical works. In the passage here he considers the weight given to the life and the death of Jesus in the writings of St Paul.*

When we talk about the life and death of our Lord Jesus Christ, we are using words in a special way. The word 'life-and-death' ought, if I may put it in that way, to be connected by hyphens; the two facts are intimately connected – indeed, you might almost say that you have a single fact there, viewed under two different aspects. Our Lord's death wasn't just the crown of his life; it was the bud of his life bursting into flower. Let me explain that phrase a little.

When somebody writes a book called *The Life and Death of Lord Nelson*, he is writing about two separate subjects. He is writing the life of a great admiral, who saved England. He is also writing about the death of a brave seaman who fell in battle. Oh, to be sure, Nelson's end was an appropriate one, from the spectacular, from the dramatic point of view. A poet could not have improved on the facts.

But Nelson's life would have been that of a great admiral, even if he had lived as long as the Duke of Wellington. And Nelson's death would have been that of a brave seaman, if he had been a simple foremast hand. Whereas in our Lord's case we know that he came to earth to die. Most of us have seen that picture of Holman Hunt's, which represents our Lord in the carpenter's shop at Nazareth, when some chance arrangement of shadows has marked the wall behind him, where he stands with outstretched arms, in the figure of a cross. I don't know whether that picture is good art, but it is good theology. Our Lord's whole life is explained and is orientated by the death he foresees.

Because the two things are so closely connected, you will find a certain difference, I will not say of opinion but of emphasis, between Christian theologians. To some, his atoning death is the only reason, as far as we know, why he came into the world at all.

The affront which our sins offered to God was infinite, and if full satisfaction was to be made for it, that could only be done by a Divine Victim; so the Second Person of the Blessed Trinity became Man and suffered, in our stead, the penalty we had deserved. That explains the Incarnation; what more could you want?

Others have laid more stress on Bethlehem, and less on Calvary; the mere fact of God taking Manhood upon him was enough of itself to heal and restore our fallen nature. They have considered it probable that there would have been an Incarnation, even if there had been no Fall.

Very roughly, you may say that the division is, as so often, a division between East and West; that it is the Latin Fathers who lay so much emphasis on the Atonement, the Greek Fathers who are more interested in the Incarnation. Very roughly, you may say that the party of the Atonement interprets the result of the Fall under a legal metaphor; the balance of the Divine justice has been disturbed, and there must be compensation before it is adjusted. Whereas the party of the Incarnation interprets the result of the Fall in organic terms; human nature has been fatally wounded, and it can only be restored by being grafted somehow into the Divine Nature; it is something like a transfusion of blood. Very roughly, you may say that one party takes its cue from our Lord's own account of his mission, 'The Son of Man came to give his life as a ransom for the lives of many' (Matthew 20.28); the other takes its cue from that other account which our Lord gave, 'I have come so that they may have life, and have it more abundantly' (John 10.10).

So the stream of Christian tradition is divided, though only, as I say, as a matter of emphasis. On which side does St Paul come down? Which party claims his support?

It would be impossible to deny that St Paul describes the work of our salvation, sometimes, under legal metaphors. You cannot, after all, speak of redemption, as St Paul often does, without using a legal metaphor. In the Old Testament almighty God is often described as redeeming his people, in a sense which generally passes over our heads. The Jewish law was very careful about hereditary titles to landed property, and if a piece of ground was up for sale, there was always somebody who had the first claim to be the purchaser, because he was the head of the family to which it originally belonged. Only if he could not or would not buy it might it be sold to a stranger; you get that prominently mentioned in the Book of Ruth. In the mind of the Hebrew prophets, ever since their deliverance from Egypt, Israel belonged specially to God, by a kind of hereditary right; and when Israel was conquered by its enemies, when its people went into exile, it meant that God's ancient inheritance was (so to speak) up for sale. Surely then he, as having the first claim upon it, would buy in this precious possession of his, instead of letting it go to strangers!

That sense of the word passes over into the New Testament, and when Zachary blesses the God of Israel for having visited his people and wrought their redemption, that sense will have been uppermost in his mind. And quite possibly St Paul, too, has it in mind when he writes to the Galatians about God sending his Son into the world to buy up those who were subject to the law (Galatians 4.5); salvation was offered first to the Jews, because God had proprietary rights over them as his own people.

But it is not merely in this vague sense of proprietorship that Jesus Christ is said to redeem us. 'A great price was paid to ransom you', St Paul writes to the Corinthians, and again, 'A price was paid to redeem you' (I Corinthians 6.20; 7.23). Here, perhaps, he is thinking of slaves being set at liberty, and drawing special attention to the fact that this can only be done by the payment of a ransom. What ransom it was that was paid to deliver us from the bondage of sin is a matter that admits of no doubt; the price paid for our liberty was a human life.

The idea of a life being given up by way of ransom was, of course, familiar to Jewish thought; it entered into the whole philosophy of sacrifice. Our Lord himself, as the first-born Son of his Mother, had to be redeemed by the slaughter of a turtledove, or two young pigeons. And he himself, as we saw just now, told us that the Son of Man came to give his life as a ransom for the lives of many – *instead* of many, if you insist on the full flavour of the word. So Paul does not imitate that turn of speech; he doesn't say that our Lord gave up his life in our stead, only that he gave it up on our behalf – perhaps a significant variation of language. We have reminded ourselves that, in St Paul's language, Christ Incarnate is the elder Brother of humanity; what a temptation for him to point to the position of the first-born in Jewish law! In theory, the first-born of every man or beast was forfeit as a sacrifice to Almighty God. In theory, then, you may say that the eldest son of a family gave up his life as a ransom for the lives of the rest; how apt a parallel that would have been! But nowhere does St Paul's language suggest it; he avoids, for the most part, the idea of a substituted Victim. Although he once refers to our Lord as a paschal Victim (I Corinthians 5.7), offered on our behalf, he never uses the word 'lamb'; it is St John and St Peter who tell us about the Lamb of God.

At the same time, you cannot deny that the death of our Lord Jesus Christ is central to St Paul's theology. He is always for drawing attention to the cross; he will make his boast of nothing else, however much the Jews shrink, however much the Gentiles mock, at the sight of its ignominy. Indeed, I think you can say that to St Paul the cross suggested, not so much the idea of suffering, as the idea of publicity. He tells the Galatians that Christ has been advertised to them, hanging on a cross (Galatians 3.1); and later in the same Epistle he says that through it the world has been crucified to him, and he to the world (6.14); it was a kind of legal instrument, setting it on record that the world has nothing to do with Paul, that Paul has nothing to do with the world, in future. Yes, a legal instrument; St Paul is never afraid of talking lawyer's language. And above all the cross is a document which sets on record the establishment of peace between God and man, like those old cairns and pillars which the patriarchs used to raise when they wanted to make a covenant. God's forgiveness means that he cancelled the deed which excluded us, the decree made to our prejudice, swept it out of the way, by nailing it to his cross (Colossians 2.14) – the cross, you see, is still the notice-board of the new covenant. A covenant of peace; it was through the cross that he abolished all feuds, including the old feud between Jew and Gentile; 'both sides, united in a single body, he would reconcile to God through his cross' (Ephesians 2.16). It was a legal instrument; you must not preach the Gospel with devices of human rhetoric, for that would be cancelling – it is the plain meaning of the word –cancelling the cross of Christ (I Corinthians 1.17).

That notion perhaps throws light on a very curious phrase used in the Epistle to the Colossians, about 'making peace through the blood of his cross' (Colossians 1.20). It is all very well to say that it simply means 'his blood shed on the cross'; but if St Paul simply meant that, it would have been easy to say that. Surely he means us to have before our eyes the picture of a cross stained with blood; surely he means us to connect it with the picture you get in the Epistle to the Hebrews, of Moses sprinkling the book with blood when he founded the old Covenant (Hebrews 9.19). Either testament was sealed with blood; the old, when Moses sprinkled the document which enshrined it, the new, when those red drops trickled down the upright wooden beam. The new covenant has the cross for its parchment, blood for its ink.

I don't mean to suggest that St Paul's thought was in any way out of harmony with our traditional Catholic doctrine of the Atonement; that he didn't look upon our Lord's death as the payment of a ransom, didn't see a foreshadowing of it in the Old Testament sacrifices. No, when Easter came round he would write to the Corinthians about Christ our paschal Victim (I Corinthians 5.7), and in his farewell speech to the elders of Ephesus he would refer to the Church as that flock which God won for himself at the price of his own blood (Acts 20.28). But that way of talking wasn't habitual with him; possibly because the old sacrifices always suggested to him the idea of substitution. Even when you offered sacrifice for a fault committed, and laid your hands on the head of the victim by way of transferring your guilt from yourself to it, that was only a kind of legal ceremony; the fact remained that you had committed a fault, and it was the goat, not you, that suffered for it. Now, we understand very little about the mystery of our redemption, and it isn't unnatural that we should represent it to ourselves as a transaction of that kind. God consented to treat our Lord's death as an expiation for our fault, although the suffering, and the acceptance of suffering, were not ours but his. The reason, I think, why St Paul didn't use that language was because it didn't match his outlook on the Incarnation. The Incarnation effected a mystical union between Christ and his Church which made it misleading to talk as if our Lord were one thing and his Church another. He didn't suffer instead of a guilty race; he identified himself, not by a legal fiction, but by a real (though mystical) union, with a guilty race, and suffered as its representative.

All through the Epistle to the Galatians, especially, this idea seems to be pressing on the mind of the Apostle, the identification of Christ with the Christian. He, Paul, has no longer any life of his own, it is Christ that lives in him; with Christ he hangs on the cross (Galatians 2.20), so that the world is crucified to him, and he to the world (6.14); he bears on his body the scars of the Crucified (6.17). And this intimate indwelling is not for a privileged few, it is general to the Christian community; the Apostle feels something like the pains of childbirth while he waits for Christ to be fully formed in his spiritual children (4.19). It is only a matter of development; already, it seems, they are Christ in embryo. 'All you who have been baptized in Christ's name have put on the person of Christ; no more Jew or Gentile, no more slave and freeman, no more male and female; you are all one person in Jesus Christ' (3.27, 28).

Bethlehem means Christ born in man, and man reborn in Christ. Calvary means that mankind has died in the person of Christ, it means also that Christ has died in the name of mankind; not instead of us, as our substitute, but in our name as our representative. He identified himself with us; I do not know where you can get clearer evidence of St Paul's view in this matter than a passage in his second letter to the Corinthians, where he argues thus: 'If one man

96

died on behalf of all, then all thereby became dead men' (50.14). If he had written 'instead of all', the argument would be nonsense; if one man dies instead of another, like Sidney Carton in the *Tale of Two Cities*, then we infer that the other man remains alive. But St Paul does not think of Christ as dying for us in that sense; rather as dying in the capacity of our representative, so that when he died we died with him. For St Paul, Christ did not die in order that we might live; he died in order that we might die. In what sense, we shall see in a moment.

It was not, then, by a kind of legal fiction that the sufferings of Jesus Christ, his, not ours, were allowed to count as reparation for our sins, ours, not his. It was in virtue of a mystical union with mankind that he was qualified to act as mankind's representative. And in this mystical sense you can even say that our guilt was transferred to him. At least it is difficult to read any other meaning into that curious verse of the Galatian Epistle, where St Paul writes: 'Those who take their stand on the law are all under a curse... From this curse invoked by the law Christ has ransomed us, by himself becoming, for our sakes, an accursed thing' (3.10, 13). There is a rather far-fetched allusion, here, to a text in Deuteronomy; we need not go into the details of all that; the fact remains that St Paul is prepared to describe our Lord as becoming 'an accursed thing'. And in writing to the Corinthians he uses an even more startling phrase: 'Christ never knew sin, and God made him into sin for us, so that in him we might be turned into the holiness of God' (II Corinthians 5.21). Christ never knew sin. It was impossible that our Lord should feel, personally, the consciousness of guilt. Yet our Lord had so identified himself with us, that what hung on the cross was, to the mystic's view, a load of guilt. To be sure, the Hebrew language made it easier for St Paul to talk like that; in Hebrew, the word for 'sin' can also be used to mean 'a victim for sin'. But the underlying sense of what St Paul says is plain enough; our Lord for our sakes became sin, so that through him we might become innocence. It is not enough to think of the cross, like the hymn *Vexilla Regis*, as a pair of scales with our sin on one side and our Lord's sacrifice on the other. We are to think of the cross as a pillory, upon which he who summed up the whole of humanity summed up the whole guilt of humanity, hung there as a kind of impersonation of guilt, and by the destruction of his body destroyed the body of our sin.

We think of our Lord's death as the meritorious cause of our deliverance from guilt; we say 'Christ died in order that we might arise again from the death of sin.' St Paul, usually though not always, thinks of Christ's death as the exemplary cause of our deliverance from guilt; he says 'Christ died, and with him and in him we died to our sins; Christ rose again, and with him and in him we rose again to a new life of innocence.' When he says 'We died to our sins', he is using language with which we are unfamiliar, but after all, as he points out, it is the language of common life. Death cancels all obligations; and we, who were debtors under the law (and bankrupt debtors, because we were bound to keep the law and we couldn't), escaped from our obligations by dying with Christ. We are dead, and our life is hidden with Christ in God; our creditor, the law of Moses, cannot get at us now.

Well, we haven't yet answered the question we set out to answer: Which school of Christian thinkers did St Paul belong to? Did he see the Incarnation as something important in itself, or as something important because of what it led up to – the Atonement? If you had put the question in that way, I don't think he would have known what to answer; because to him the Atonement was part of the Incarnation, one aspect of it, one mood of it, not to be isolated in contrast with the rest. 'All I know', he would have told you, 'is that when Jesus Christ became Man, you and I were somehow mystically identified with him. His life, not just by the circumstances of it but by the whole purpose and dedication of it, led up to his death on the cross. And when he died, you and I, mystically identified with him, became dead to our old life of sin and disobedience; we were buried with him, and rose again with him into a new life, in which God is our sun and Christ is the air we breathe. Was it the Incarnation, or the Atonement, that did that? I cannot tell; all I know is that my life is "the faith I have in the Son of God, who loved me, and gave himself for me".'

# God's face
# John Donne

*John Donne (1572–1631) made as daring use of 'metaphysical' conceits in his poetry as anyone, but they succeed. If none of his poetry had survived, his astonishing powers of language would have shone from the sermons he gave as Dean of St Paul's in the last ten years of his life, except that most people do not read sermons. Donne writes in his poetry of fleshly love as burningly as of godly realities: death, prayer, suffering, love too.*

*For this poem it is useful to know that Donne was aware of the idea of planets being governed and moved by celestial intelligences – angels, as we might call them. The planets and stars moved in, as it were, concentric invisible spheres, each influenced by the next sphere out from it. Surrounding all was the* primum mobile, *given its all-governing motion by God, the unmoved mover. The cosmic order pervades the whole poem, but as it proceeds the emphasis is increasingly on the poet's own relationship with the crucified Christ.*

## Goodfriday, 1613. Riding Westward

Let man's Soule be a Spheare, and then, in this,
The intelligence that moves, devotion is,
And as the other Spheares, by being growne
Subject to forraigne motions, lose their owne,
And being by others hurried every day,
Scarce in a yeare their natural forme obey:
Pleasure or businesse, so, our Soules admit
For their first mover, and are whirld by it.
Hence is't, that I am carryed towards the West
This day, when my Soule's forme bends toward the East.
There I should see a Sunne, by rising set,
And by that setting endlesse day beget;
But that Christ on this Crosse, did rise and fall,

Sinne had eternally benighted all.
Yet dare I almost be glad, I do not see
That spectacle of too much weight for mee.
Who sees God's face, that is selfe life, must dye;
What a death were it then to see God dye?
It made his owne Lieutenant Nature shrinke,
It made his footstoole crack, and the Sunne winke.
Could I behold those hands which span the Poles,
And turne all spheares at once, pierc'd with those holes?
Could I behold that endlesse height which is
Zenith to us, and our Antipodes,
Humbled below us? or that blood which is
The seat of all our Soules, if not of his,
Made durt of dust, or that flesh which was worne
By God, for his apparell, rag'd, and torne?
If on these things I durst not looke, durst I
Upon his miserable mother cast mine eye,
Who was God's partner here, and furnish'd thus
Halfe of that Sacrifice, which ransom'd us?
Though these things, as I ride, be from mine eye;
They're present yet unto my memory,
For that looks towards them; and thou look'st towards mee,
O Saviour, as thou hang'st upon the tree;
I turne my backe to thee, but to receive
Corrections, till thy mercies bid thee leave.
O thinke mee worth thine anger, punish mee,
Burne off my rusts, and my deformity,
Restore thine Image, so much, by thy grace,
That thou may'st know mee, and I'll turne my face.

# 18

## Word made flesh
## Rowan Williams

*Rowan Williams (born 1950) is a theologian (Lady Margaret Professor of Divinity at Oxford, 1986–92), and his theological writing is sometimes constrained by the requirement not to speak out beyond the discipline of the science. But even in* On Christian Theology *(Blackwell, 2000) he repeatedly makes clear his commitment in faith to Christian belief and worship. He was named Archbishop of Canterbury in 2002.*

*In the passage below from his historical survey of Christian spirituality,* The Wound of Knowledge *(Darton, Longman & Todd, 1979), he outlines Irenaeus's attempt to distinguish the false use of information offered by the gnostic heretics from the living use of an historical encounter embraced by Christians.*

Christian opponents of gnosticism had a good deal to say about the reduction of salvation to spiritual technology. Irenaeus of Lyons (c.130–c.200), in his major work *Against the Heresies (Adversus Haereses)*, devotes a long section of the second book to a consideration of the difficult question of God's distinctness from 'nature', *physis*, and therefore from any kind of determined process.

The problem, of course, is to state such a distinctness without capitulating to the very view being contradicted. Gnosticism proposes a radical division between an order of bodily nature and an order of spiritual nature: Irenaeus has to set nature, bodily and spiritual, over against the total gratuity of God's dealing with men, and yet avoid a devaluation of this 'nature'. He makes it quite clear that salvation is not 'natural' to the soul, natural in the sense of being potentially within the control of the spiritual side of man, needing only enlightenment to be realized. Salvation is a relationship of love with God, initiated by God's free choice, available to the person living in 'righteousness'. Communion with God is a 'reward' for righteous living: that is to say, God will give himself to the righteous, but righteousness is not itself simply identical with communion.

There is no sort of human activity which *automatically* generates the vision of God, but there are actions which make one 'apt' for the vision of God. And these are, as Irenaeus vehemently insists, the acts of the whole person: 'the things which are proper to righteousness are brought to completion in the body'. The life of the soul in itself is nothing. Sense experience, reflection, volition are all matters involving more than the soul; soul and body are inseparably bound together, and the soul would have no individuality or identity independently of the body.

For Irenaeus, then, there can be no single 'spiritual' history: God does not have a history, since he does not belong to the order of natural interaction and causality; and man has no history apart from his fleshly existence, in all its contingency and variety. Where the gnostics had pressed God and *nous* together in one spiritual *genos*, Irenaeus forces them apart. He does not deny the unfreedom of the empirical human condition; but unlike the gnostics, he attributes this to the human failure to fulfil the original purposes of God for mankind in history.

Man is created in God's image – created with the capacity for relationship to God in obedience: his fulfilment is in this relationship. 'The life of man is the vision of God.' But the image is potential only, it must be made into a 'likeness' by the exercise of goodness. Had man been created in perfection, he would have performed his good acts automatically; and God requires man freely to create in his life the pattern of right action. God's will, in fact, is for humanity to make its own history, and within that history to grow towards a sharing in his life. 'The real subsistence of life comes from sharing in God: and this sharing in God means seeing God and enjoying his generosity.' It is here that humanity has failed, refusing to grow, and so condemning itself to imperfect

102

and insubstantial life, subject to 'corruption' – the tendency to disintegration, instability, chaos and, ultimately, death, bodily and spiritual. The whole man has been called to realize the likeness of God, and the whole man has failed and is in need of healing.

The only history to be taken seriously is bodily history; and so the redemption of man must be located in bodily history. The gnostics regarded the Old Testament as a grotesque embarrassment, the record of a nation bound to crude and superstitious beliefs about God's involvement with creation. Irenaeus insists upon the *continuity* of God's activity: the redemptive act is spread over a great length of time in Israel's history, and it is the same God who is at work in the patriarchs and prophets as in Christ.

God makes himself known in vision and 'mystery' to the Jews, and in the words and deeds of the prophets. It is interesting to find Irenaeus drawing attention to the 'prophetic sign', the symbolic acts (and even lives) of such as Isaiah, Jeremiah, Ezekiel and Hosea, as an important means of God's communication to men. Characteristically, attention is being drawn away from words and ideas to the 'speech' of historical fact. In the Old Covenant God reveals himself under Law and prophecy to enjoin righteousness upon men. By their obedience they may come to true vision of God, and so to share in his life in some degree.

Yet in the Old Covenant there remains a distance between humanity and the God who, although he speaks, remains invisible. If man is to share the life of God, to 'enter into God', God must not only speak but enter humanity; and the prophetic revelation can never go so far. Man, created to be 'the glory of God', has deprived himself and his world of freedom by Adam's yielding to temptation; he can no longer *create* in his life the icon of God's beauty. So if he is to be restored, no worldly agency can effect his healing, nor can any power outside him. The healing must be enacted in human flesh by the only one who is truly free, the creator himself.

Thus the absolute distinction between creator and creation which is fundamental to Irenaeus' anti-gnostic argument is overcome by the divine freedom to act in man's history; but to act in history is to act as man, so that the distinction must, at one level, remain absolute. The re-creator can only act as a creature, not as a creator external to the world's history. Thus, in the person of 'the Redeemer', we know God not 'according to His greatness', *secundum magnitudinem*, but 'according to His love', *secundum dilectionem*.

This is not to draw the kind of distinction which later Eastern theologians were to develop between God's 'substance' and his 'operations', but simply to underline the truth that saving knowledge of God is a relationship initiated by God's free decision to love, to delight in, his creation, by his *dilectio*. It is not a vision of majesty or transcendence for us to admire from a distance; it is the encounter with God in the world. We do not *see* the *magnitudo*, and we cannot understand the 'nature' of God. The gnostic error is to assume that such a detached and impersonal knowledge is healing and reconciling, when it is not even possible.

We have seen the incomprehensible Father only in the Son, in a compassion which heals, renews and enlarges our hearts, teaching us that our mortal existence can be transfigured to the likeness of Christ who is the likeness of the unseen Father. 'For when the Word of God was made flesh, He established both these things: He showed us the true image [of God in man] by Himself becoming what was in fact His own image; and He established and restored the likeness [of man to God] by making man resemble the invisible Father by means of [His action as] the visible Word.'

This is neatly summed up in a phrase when Irenaeus calls the Son the *gnosis* of the Father: the Father's relationship with the Son is the paradigm of knowledge, the Father knows and is known by the communion he enjoys with the Son. So to know God through or in the Son is to know in communion or 'community of union': it is to possess the Spirit of adoption whereby we have a foretaste of our future relationship with the Father in being enabled to cry 'Abba'.

# Salve sancta facies

*An anonymous prayer of the fourteenth century, found in manuscript.*

All hail! the holy face of our Againbuyer, in whom shineth the image of heavenly shining, made in a coverchief as white as snow, given to Veronica for token of love. All hail! the worship of the world, the mirror of saints, whom spirits of heaven covet for to see. Cleanse us from every spot of vice and join us to the fellowship of blessed men. All hail! our joy in this hard life, sliding and breakable, soon for to pass. Ah thou blessed face lead us to a country, to Christ's face to be seen, that is full clear. We beseech, be to us a siker [sure] helper, a sweet defender, and a counsellor that a grievous enemy noye [trouble] us not, but enjoy we rest.

All folk say they: 'So be it.'

# 19

# Fire and mercy
# William Sancroft

*William Sancroft (1617–1693) was Dean of St Paul's when it was burned down in the Great Fire of London in 1666. His sermon on the incident, 'Lex Ignea, or the School of Righteousness', from which the passage below is taken, was preached before Charles II on 10 October, a month after the fire, but gained a much wider audience through publication. His successor, William Tillotson, was credited with introducing a clear, plain style of prose, but Sancroft was no mean stylist himself.*

*Sancroft was a learned man of the same religious attitude as William Laud or Lancelot Andrewes, and himself became Archbishop of Canterbury. But public events had repeatedly put him in hard positions. As a young man during the Commonwealth he had to leave Emmanuel College, Cambridge, where he was a fellow, and go abroad. After the Great Fire his generosity aided the rebuilding of St Paul's, but the accession of James II in 1685 spelled trouble, since the new king was Roman Catholic. Sancroft crowned him according to the established rite, omitting the Communion. Sancroft was one of the Seven Bishops tried for seditious libel and acquitted under James, but the coming in of William II in his place proved no relief, for Sancroft was among those convinced they were unable to swear an oath to the new king while the old one lived, and he found himself a leader of the non-juring bishops. Archbishop Tillotson was installed in his stead in 1691, and Sancroft retired quietly to the Suffolk village where he had been brought up, dying two years later. Tillotson survived him for one year, attended at his death by the commentator on the Book of Common Prayer, Robert Nelson – by an historic irony a non-juror.*

When a judgement is particular and reacheth but a few, we have a savage promptness in condemning the Sufferers, with, 'This is God's just Judgement for such a thing.' So long as the Thunder-bolt flies over our own Heads, we hug ourselves, and All is well; 'tis our dear pastime, and a high voluptuousness to sit and censure others, and flatter our selves, that we are more righteous than they. To meet with this ill Humour, God hath reacht us now an universal stroak that comes home to every Man: So that 'tis as Isaiah states, 'As with the Prince and the Priest, so with the people, as with the Master and the Mistress, so with the Servant, as with the Buyer and the Borrower, so with the Seller and the Lender.' In fine, He is no Englishman that feels not this Blow: And therefore as the judgement is Universal, let us give Glory to God, and confess, that the Sin is so too; saying with the good Nehemiah, 'Thou art just, O God, in All that is brought upon us; on our King; and on our Princes; on our Priests, and on our Prophets; on our Fathers, and on all thy People; For thou hast done Right, but we have All done Wickedly.' God give us Grace to take every one the shame that belongs properly to himself, and to join heartily together in a full Chorus at the last, repeating that excellent Exomologesis of holy David, with which I conclude this point, 'Righteous art thou, O Lord, and are thy judgements.' But there is another yet behind —

Lastly, give God the Glory of his Mercy too; that must in no wise be forgotten. 'Tis the privilege and prerogative of Mercy, that it mixeth itself in all God's Works; even in justice it self too. 'He sendeth forth Lightnings with the Rain' saith the Psalmist. 'He bringeth the Winds out of his Treasuries.' Strange Furniture, one would think for a Treasury, Storms and Tempests! But there is so very much of Mercy even in God's judgements too, that they also deserve a place amongst his Treasures, ay and amongst ours too. For he licenseth not a Wind, or a Storm, lets not fly a flash of Lightning, or a Ball of Fire, but a Mercy goes along with it; comes flying to us (if we miss it not by our Negligence or Inadvertency) upon the Wings of that Wind; and discovers it self to us even by the Light of those Fires. And therefore turn not away your Eyes in Horror, but study the late Conflagration: And even in the Dust and Ashes of our City, if we sift and examine them well, we may find rich Treasures of Mercy hidden.

Mercy first, that God spar'd us, and preserv'd us so long. For without his Divine Manutenency, our strongest Fabricks had faln immediately upon their very Builders. He that made all things at first, by preserving makes them still; new makes them every Moment; and for his Will's sake alone they were and are created. He carries Nature always in his Bosom, fostering and cherishing her; and that not only as she came out of his own hand and bears the Impresses of his Infinite Wisdom and Power; but as we have transform'd and disguised her by our petty skill; as she is fettered and shackled by our silly Artifices: Even the World of Fancy too, the poor attempts and Bunglings of Art, our Houses of Dirt and Clay (which we call Palaces and so please ourselves in) would quickly fall asunder, and moulder all into the Dust they consist of, did not an Almighty Hand uphold them. If he keep not the House and the City, in vain the Builder builds, and the Watchman wakes, and the Centinel stands *perdu*. And therefore give we him the Glory of this Mercy, saying, 'Thanks be to the Lord, who so long shew'd

107

us marvellous great Kindness.' I say not with the Psalm, 'in a strong City' (though the strongest without him is weakness), but in a very weak One: A City in the Meanness of the Materials, the Oldness of the Buildings, the streightess of some Streets, the ill Situation of others, and many like Inconveniencies, so expos'd to this dismal Accident, that it must needs have been long since in Ashes, had not his miraculous Mercy preserv'd it, who, so long as he pleaseth (and that is just so long as we please him) continues the Fire to us useful and safe, serviceable, and yet innocent, with as much ease as he lays it asleep, and quiet in the Bosom of a Flint.

Mercy again, That he afflicts us at all; that we are yet in his School; that he hath not quite given us over, and turned us out as unteachable and incorrigible. 'Felix cui Deus dignatur irasci', saith Tertullian; in David's Language, 'Blessed is the Man whom thou chastnest O Lord, and teachest him in thy Law'; send'st him thy judgements, and learn'st him thy Righteousness. But to sin, and not be punished is the sorest punishment of all, saith Saint Chrysostome. 'Dimisit eos secundum desideria Cordis'. He suffered them to walk after their own Heart's Lusts, that's a dreadful portion: 'Let them alone, Why should they be stricken any more?' that's 'the prosperity of Fools that destroys them', as Solomon; or as David phraseth it. This is for God 'to rain Snares upon the ungodly: A horrible Tempest indeed!' as he there calls it, and worse than the Fire and Brimstone in the same Verse.

Mercy too, That he afflicts us himself, keeps us still under his own Discipline, and hath 'not yet given us over unto the Will of our Adversaries'. The hand of an Enemy poysons the Wound: His Malice or his Insolence doubles and trebles the Vexation. The Malignity of the Instrument may invenom a Scratch into a Gangrene: But the Blessed Hand of God, even when it strikes, drops Balsom. His very Rods are bound up in Silk and softness, and dipt beforehand in Balm: He wounds that he may heal, and in wounding heals: 'Una, eademque Manus Vulnus, opemque' – And therefore may we never be beaten by the hand of a cruel and insulting Slave: But let our Righteous Lord himself 'smite us, and it shall be a kindness; let him correct us, and it shall be an excellent Oyl. O let us still fall into the Hands of God (for great are his Mercies) but let us not fall into the hands of Men.'

Mercy lastly in the Degree of the Affliction; That he hath punished us less than our Iniquities deserve; afflicted us in measure; corrected us in Judgement, not in his Fury, for then we had been utterly brought to nothing: That we have had our Lives for a Prey, and are as so many Fire-brands pluckt out of the Burning. And therefore, why should a living Man complain? Say we rather as Abraham did in the Case of Sodom, when he had that horrible Scene of Vengeance now in his Eye, 'We are but Dust and Ashes': Not only Dust in the course of ordinary Frailty, but Ashes too in the merit of a far sharper Doom; deserve, that God should bring us to Dust, nay, even turn us to Ashes too, as our Houses. 'It is of the Lord's Mercies, that We ourselves also are not consumed because his compassions fail not'; that any part of our City is still remaining; that God hath left us yet a holy place to assemble in, solemnly to acknowledge (as we do this Day) his most miraculous Mercy: That when all our Wit was puzzl'd, and all our Industry tired out; when the Wind was at the highest, and the Fire at the hottest, and all our hopes were now giving up the Ghost, Then He, whose season is our greatest extremity; He, who 'stayeth his rough Wind in the Day of the East-wind'; He, who alone sets Bounds to the Rage of the Waters; restrain'd also on the suddain, the Fury of this other merciless and unruly Element, by the Interposition of his Almighty *Hucusque*, hitherto shalt thou go, and no further. Ay this deserves indeed to be the Matter of a Song, Joy in the Lord upon so great an Occasion, upon so noble an Experience, sits not unhandsome on the Brow of so sad a Day as this is. 'It shall be said in that Day', saith our Prophet (and let us all say it; say it with Triumph, and jubilee too), 'Lo, this is our God, we have waited for him, and He hath saved us; This is the Lord, we will be glad, and rejoyce in his Salvation.'

# Fiery, cloudy pillar
## William Williams and Peter Williams

*William Williams (1719–91) and Peter Williams (1722–96) were unrelated. Both were Methodists. Peter Williams helped William Williams translate this hymn from Welsh. As first published in 1771, the hymn began 'Guide me, O Thou great Jehovah'.*

Guide me, O Thou great redeemer,
   Pilgrim through this barren land;
I am weak, but Thou art mighty,
   Hold me with Thy powerful hand;
      Bread of Heaven,
      Bread of Heaven,
Feed me now and evermore.

Open now the crystal fountain
   Whence the healing streams do flow;
Let the fiery, cloudy pillar
   Lead me all my journey through;
      Strong Deliverer,
      Strong Deliverer,
Be Thou still my Strength and Shield.

When I tread the verge of Jordan,
   Bid my anxious fears subside:
Death of death and hell's Destruction,
   Land me safe on Canaan's side;
      Songs of praises,
      Songs of praises,
I will ever give to Thee. Amen.

# 20

# Faith means thanks
# William Law

*William Law (1686–1761) is best known for his* Serious Call to a
Devout and Holy Life *(see Introduction), which caught the imagination of
the age with its accurate delineation of character types, and inspired a deep
change in many who read it.*

*Law was one of eleven children of a grocer, and remained all his life
connected with his birthplace, Kings Cliffe, Northamptonshire. He took orders
but would not swear the oath when George I succeeded to the throne. Thus
debarred from office, he became a tutor, to the father of Edward Gibbon.
With some inheritance and the earnings from his books, he set up a school and
from 1740 lived a regular life of piety and charity, in accord with the* Serious
Call, *with his brother's widow and Edward Gibbon's aunt, Hester, who had
between them a very good income. Much went to relieve the poor, and Law was
once denounced for his indiscriminate generosity by the local rector from the
pulpit.*

*Law's fondness for the mysticism of Jacob Boehme confirmed a breach with
Wesley, who had been an early follower. Law enjoyed singing. He also had a
natural sympathy for animals, and disliked them being caged up.*

A dull, uneasy, complaining spirit, which is sometimes the spirit of
those that seem careful of Religion, is yet, of all tempers, the most
contrary to Religion, for it disowns that God which it pretends to
adore. For he sufficiently disowns God, who does not adore him as a
Being of infinite goodness.

If a man does not believe that all the world is as God's family,
where nothing happens by chance, but all is guided and directed by
the care and providence of a Being that is all love and goodness to
all his creatures; if a man do not believe this from his heart, he

cannot be said truly to believe in God. And yet he that has this faith, has faith enough to overcome the world, and always be thankful to God. For he that believes that everything happens to him for the best, cannot possibly complain for the want of something that is better.

If therefore you live in murmurings and complaints, accusing all the accidents of life, it is not because you are a weak, infirm creature, but it is because you want the first principle of religion, a right belief in God. For as thankfulness is an express acknowledgment of the goodness of God towards you, so repinings and complaints, are as plain accusations of God's want of goodness towards you.

On the other hand, would you know who is the greatest Saint in the world: It is not he who prays most, or fasts most; it is not he who gives most alms, or is most eminent for temperance, chastity, or justice; but it is he who is always thankful to God, who wills everything that God willeth, who receives everything as an instance of God's goodness, and has a heart always ready to praise God for it.

All prayer and devotion, fastings and repentance, meditation and retirement, all sacraments and ordinances, are but so many means to render the soul thus divine and conformable to the will of God, and to fill it with thankfulness and praise for everything that comes from God. This is the perfection of all virtues; and all virtues that do not tend to it, or proceed from it, are but so many false ornaments of a soul not converted unto God.

# Elemental instruments
## Queen Elizabeth I

*Elizabeth I's prayer of thanks on the defeat of the Spanish Armada, September 1588.*

Everlasting and omnipotent Creator, Redeemer and Conserver, when it seemed most fit time to Thy worthy providence to bestow the workmanship of this world or globe with Thy rare judgement, Thou didst divide into four singular parts the form of all this mold, which aftertime hath termed elements, they all serving to continue in orderly government the whole of all the mass; which all, when of Thy most singular bounty and never-earst-seen care Thou hast this year made serve for instruments both to daunt our foes and to confound their malice. I most humbly, with bowed heart and bended knees, do render my humblest acknowledgements and lowliest thanks; and not the least for that the weakest sex hath been so fortified by Thy strongest help that neither my people might find lack by my weakness nor foreigners triumph at my ruin. Such hath been Thy unwonted grace in my days, although Satan hath never made holiday in busy practices both for my life and state, yet that Thy mighty hand hath overspread both with shade of Thy blessed wings so that both neither hath been overthrown nor received shame but obtained victory to Thy most great glory and their greatest ignomy; for which, Lord, of Thy mere goodness grant us grace to be hourly thankful and ever mindful. And if it may please Thee to pardon my request, give us the continuance in my days of like goodness, that mine eyes never see change of such grace to me, but specially to this my kingdom, which, Lord, grant to flourish many ages after my end. Amen.

21

# God's thirst
## Julian of Norwich

*Julian of Norwich (1342–1413) was an anchoress, living in a fixed place, probably a little room attached to a church, spending her time in prayer. Her Revelations of Divine Love fitted in with the tradition of English spirituality of the time. In it she sometimes refers to St Dionyse of France, which she thought was the identity of the Pseudo-Dionysius (see Introduction), through a general confusion between Dionysius and St Denis, the patron of France.*

*Dame Julian was admired in her day (the neurotic Margery Kempe going to visit her and being given a listening ear and sound advice) and has been ever since because of the obvious goodness of her approach. She does not write as a theologian but as a mystic.*

*In the translation used here, 'ghostly' means 'spiritual', and 'in my sight' means 'as I see it'.*

## Of the longing and the ghostly thirst of Christ, which lasteth and shall last till Doomsday; and by reason of his body he is not yet fully glorified, nor all impassible

And thus our good Lord answered to all the questions and doubts that I might make, saying full comfortably: 'I may make all thing well, I can make all thing well, I will make all thing well, and I shall make all thing well; and thou shalt see thyself that all manner of thing shall be well.'

In that he saith: 'I may', I understand it for the Father; and in that he saith, 'I can', I understand it for the Son; and where he saith: 'I will', I understand it for the Holy Ghost; and where he saith: 'I shall', I understand it for the unity of the blessed Trinity: three Persons and one Truth; and where he saith: 'Thou shalt see thyself', I understand the oneing of all mankind that shall be saved unto the blessed Trinity. And in these five words God willeth we be enclosed in rest and in peace.

Thus shall the ghostly Thirst of Christ have an end. For this is the ghostly Thirst of Christ: the love-longing that lasteth and ever shall, till we see that sight on Doomsday. For we that shall be saved and shall be Christ's joy and his bliss, some be yet here and some be to come, and so shall some be, unto that day. Therefore this is his thirst and love-longing, to have us altogether whole in him, in his bliss, – as to my sight. For we be not now as fully whole in him as we shall be then.

For we know in our Faith, and also it was shewed in all the

Shewings that Christ Jesus is both God and man. And anent [concerning] the Godhead, he is himself highest bliss, and was from without beginning, and shall be, without end; which endless bliss may never be heightened nor lowered in itself. For this was plenteously seen in every Shewing, and specially in the Twelfth, where he saith: 'I am that which is highest.'

And anent Christ's Manhood, it is known in our Faith, and also it was shewed, that he, with the virtue of Godhead, for love to bring us to his bliss, suffered pains and passions and died. And these be the works of Christ's Manhood wherein he rejoiceth; and that shewed he in the Ninth Shewing, where he saith: 'It is a joy and bliss and endless pleasing that ever I suffered Passion for thee.' And this is the bliss of Christ's works, and thus he meaneth where he saith in that same Shewing; we be his bliss, we be his meed [reward], we be his worship, we be his crown.

For as Christ is our Head, he is glorified and impassible; and anent his Body in which all his members be knit, he is not yet fully glorified nor all impassible. Therefore the same desire and thirst that he had upon the cross (which desire, longing, and thirst, as to my sight, was in him from without beginning) the same hath he yet, and shall have unto the time that the last soul that shall be saved is come up to his bliss.

For as verily as there is a property in God of ruth [mercy, or sympathy] and pity, so verily there is a property in God of thirst and longing. (And of the virtue of this longing in Christ, we have to long again to Him: without which no soul cometh to Heaven.) And this property of longing and thirst cometh of the endless Goodness of God, right as the property of pity cometh of his endless Goodness. And though longing and pity are two sundry properties as to my sight, in this standeth the point of the ghostly Thirst: which is lasting in him as long we be in need, drawing us up to his bliss. And all this was seen in the Shewing of Compassion: for that shall cease on Doomsday.

Thus he hath ruth and compassion on us, and he hath longing to have us; but his wisdom and his love suffereth not the end to come till the best time.

115

# PART 3

# *Responding to God*

# 22

# The mystical bee
# Francis de Sales

*Francis de Sales (1567–1622), a Frenchman who became Bishop of Geneva, held a particular appeal for English lay people. In his* Introduction to the Devout Life *he did not ask laity to leave their ordinary way of life (while more clerical spiritual writers denounced dancing, for example, as a sin). He explained how to practise daily prayer and integrate a life of piety with the demands of a trade, profession or family commitments. In* The Love of God *he uses the same curious analogies from natural history that made his* Introduction *attractive. The imaginary interlocutor to whom meditation is explained is called Theophila (Theo).*

*In the passage given here, the translation is the first made into English, published in 1630 under the pen-name Miles Car by Miles Pinkney (1599–1674), a friend of the poet Richard Crashaw.*

## Of Meditation, the first degree of Prayer or mysticall Divinitie

Every *Meditation* is a thought, but every thought is not *Meditation*, for we have thoughtes to which our mind is caried without aime or pretention at all, by way of a simple musing, as we see flies flie from one flowere to an other, without drawing anything from them: And be this kind of thought as attentive as it may be, it can never beare the name of *Meditation*; but must be called a simple thought. Sometimes we consider a thinge attentively to learne its causes, effectes, qualities; and this thought is named studie, in which the mind is like locustes, which promiscuously flie upon flowres and leaves, to eate them and nourishe themselfes thereupon. But when we thinke of heavenly things, not to learne but to love them, that is called, to *Meditate*; and the exercise thereof *Meditation* in which our mind, not as a flie, by a simple musing, nor yet as a locust, to eate and be filled, but as a sacred Bee flies amongst the flowres of holy mysteries, to extract from them the honie of Divine Love.

So divers men are alwayes dreaming and busying themselves in unprofitable thoughtes, without knowing in a manner what they thinke upon and which is admirable, they are onely attentive for want of attention, and would be rid of such thoughtes. Wittnesse he that saied: My thoughtes waste themselves, tormenting my heart. Others there are that studie, and by a most laborious trade, fill themselves with vanitie, not being able to withstand curiositie. But few there are, that meditate, to kindle their heart with heavenly love. In fine, thoughtes and studies may be upon any subject, but meditation in our present sense hath reference onely to those objectes whose consideration tends to make us good and devote. So that meditation is an attentive thought iterated, or voluntarily intertained in the mind, to excite the will to holy affections and resolutions.

Verily the holy word doth admirably well explicate by an excellent similitude wherein holy meditation consisteth. Ezechias when he would explicate in his Canticle the attentive consideration which he had of his annoyes [troubles]: 'I will crie', saieth he, 'like a young swallow, and meditate as a dove.' For, my deare Theo: if ever you tooke notice of it, the younge swallows doe gape wide in their chirping, and contrariwise, the dove, of all the birdes doth murmur with her neb shut and clos'd, rowling her voice in her weesell and crope, nothing passing outwardly but a certaine resounding or echo-like sound and this close murmuring doth equally serve her in the expression of her griefe and loves.

Ezechias then to shew, that in his calamitie he made many vocall Prayers: 'I will crie'' saieth he, 'as a younge swallow, opening my mouth, to lay before God in many lamentable voices'; and to testifie also that he made use of holy mentall prayer, he addes, 'I will meditate, as a dove winding and doubling my thoughtes within my

120

heart, by an attentive consideration, to excite my selfe to blisse and praise the soveraigne mercy of my God, who hath broughte me backe from death's gate, taking compassion of my miserie.'

So saieth Isaie, 'We will roare or rustle like Beares, and meditating we will mourne as Doves.' The rustling of Beares doth resemble the exclamations which are made in vocall prayer, and the mourning of Doves is compared to holy meditation. But to the end it may appeare that Doves doe not onely mourne in occasions of griefe, but even of love also and joye, the sacred Spouse describing the naturall spring-time, to expresse the graces of the spiritual spring-time: 'The Turtle's voice', saieth he, 'hath been heard in our land', because in the spring the Turtle begins to waxe hote with love: which by her most frequent song she testifieth. And presently after, 'My Dove, shew me thy face, let thy voice resound in my eares; for thy voice is sweete, and thy face comely and gracious.' He would saie, Theo: that the devote soule is most agreeable unto him, when she presents her selfe before him, and meditates to heate her selfe in holy spirituall love, as doe Doves to stirre up their mates to a naturall love. So he that had saied, 'I will meditate as a Dove', putting his conceite into other words, 'I will recall to mind', saieth he, 'all my yeares in the bitternesse of my soule.' For to meditate; and to recall to mind to th'end to move affection, are the same thing. Hence Moyses exhorting the people to recall to mind the benefits received of God, he adds this reason, 'To th'end you may observe his commandements, walke in his wayes, and fear him.' And our Saviour himselfe gave this command to Josue: 'Thou shalt meditate in the book of the lawe, day and night, that thereby thou mayest observe and doe that which is written in it'; which in one of the passages, is expressed by the word *Meditate*, is declared in the other, by *Recall to Mind*.

And to shew that an iterated thought and meditation tend to move us to affections, resolutions and actions; it is saied as well in the one as the other passage, that we must recall to mind, and meditate in the Law, to observe and practise it. In this sense the Apostle exhorts us saying, 'Think diligently upon him who

121

sustained of sinners such contradiction against himselfe, that you be not wearied, fainting in your minds.' When he saieth 'think diligently', it is as though he had saied 'meditate'. But why would he have us so to meditate the holy passion? Not that we should waxe learned, but that we should become patient, and constant in the way of heaven.

Meditation is a mystical ruminating requisite that we might not be found uncleane, to which one of the pious shepherdesses that followeth the sacred Sunamite invites us; for she assures us that holy writ is as a precious wine, worthy to be drunk not onely by the Pastours and Doctours, but also to be diligently tasted, chewed and ruminated, as one would saie. 'Thy throte', saieth she, 'wherein the holy words are formed, is a best wine worthy of my well-beloved, to be drunk with his lippes, and ruminated with his teeth.' So the Blessed Isaac, as a neate and pure Lambe, towards night went out into the fields, to recollect, conferre, and exercise his Spirit with God, that is, to pray and meditate.

The Bee flies from flowre to flowre in the spring time, not at all adventures, but of pourpose, not to be recreated onely in the verdant diapring [pattern] of the fieldes, but to gather honie, which having found, she sucks and lodes her selfe with it, thence carying it to her hyve, she accommodates it artificially, separating the waxe from it, therof makeing the combe to reserve honie for the ensuing winter. Such is the devote soule in meditation; she passeth from mysterie to mysterie, not at randome, or to solace her selfe onely in viewing the admirable beautie of those divine objectes but deliberatly and of set pourpose, to find out motifes of love, or some heavenly affection. And having found them, she drawes them to her, she relisheth them and lodes her selfe with them, and having brought them home, and placed them in her heart, she selectes that which she finds most proper for her advancement, storing herselfe with fit resolutions against the time of temptation.

Thus the celestiall Spouse as a mystical bee flies to the Canticle of

Canticles now upon the eyes, now upon the lippes, cheekes and head haire of the well-beloved, to draw from thence the sweetnesse of a thousand passions of love; to this effect noting in particular whatsoever she finds rare. So that inflamed with holy love, she speakes with him, puts interrogatories to him. She harkes, sighes, aspires, admires; as he of his part fills her with delight, inspiring her, touching and opening her heart and streaming into it brightnesse, lighte, and sweetenesses without end, but in so secrete a manner, that one may rightly saie of this holy conversation of the soule with God, as the Holy Text saieth of God's with Moises, that Moises being sole upon the top of the mountaine, he spoke to God, and God answered him.

# Nothing dark
## Catechism of Edward VI

*The Catechism of Edward VI was issued in 1553 with instructions that it should be used by all schoolmasters. It was intended to consolidate the effects of the Prayer Book of the preceding year. The Catechism, in Latin and English versions, circulated only in small numbers before Edward died and Mary came to the throne.*

MASTER.  Hast thou any certain and appointed manner of praying?

SCHOLAR.  Yea forsooth: even the very same, that our Lord taught his disciples, and in them all other Christians. Who, being on a time required to teach them some sort of prayer, taught them this. When you pray, quoth he, say: 'Our Father which art in heaven, hallowed be thy name. Thy kingdom come. Thy will be done in earth as it is in heaven. Give us this day our daily bread, and forgive us our trespasses as we forgive them that trespass against us. And lead us not into temptation: But deliver us from evil. For thine is the kingdom, power and glory for ever. Amen.'

MASTER.   How thinkest thou? is it lawful for us to use any other words of prayer?

SCHOLAR.   Although in this short abridgment are sufficiently contained all things that every Christian ought to pray for: yet hath not Christ in this prayer tied us up so short, as that it were not lawful for us to use other words and manner of prayer. But he hath set out in this prayer certain principal points, whereunto all our prayers should be referred. But let each man ask of God as his present need requireth. 'Whatsoever ye ask the Father in my name', saith Christ, 'he shall give it you.'

MASTER.   Forasmuch as there is in all this prayer nothing doubtful or beside the purpose: I would hear thy mind of it.

SCHOLAR.   I do well perceive what the words do signify.

MASTER.   Thinkest thou then that there is in it nothing dark, nothing hid, nothing hard to understand?

SCHOLAR.   Nothing at all. For neither was it Christ's pleasure, that there should be any thing in it dark or far from our capacity, specially since it belongeth equally to all, and is as necessary for the lewd, as the learned.

23

# Dark hiding place
# John of the Cross

*John of the Cross (1542–91) joined Teresa of Avila in the reform of the Carmelite order. For his trouble he was imprisoned by his own religious brothers – a hard physical ordeal, but a far more distressing emotional experience. He made a providential escape and continued his work.*

*For John, sincere perseverance in prayer is the one thing necessary. He is a reliable guide to mental prayer, the prayer that God ordinarily grants people who attempt it. His 'dark night', painful perhaps but not unwelcome, expresses one effect of the infinite God on limited humanity. John was a poet too, which gives his exposition depth. In this extract from his commentary on his own* Spiritual Canticle, *he stresses the whole point of prayer: attention to Jesus.*

You do very well, O soul, to seek him ever as one hidden, for you exalt God and approach very near him when you consider him higher and deeper than anything you can reach. Hence pay no attention, either partially nor entirely, to anything your faculties can grasp. I mean that you should never seek satisfaction in what you understand about God, but in what you do not understand about him. Never pause to love and delight in your understanding and experience of God, but love and delight in what you cannot understand or experience of him. Such is the way, as we said, of seeking him in faith. However surely it may seem that you find, experience, and understand God, because he is inaccessible and concealed you must always regard him as hidden, and serve him who is hidden in a secret way. Do not be like the many foolish ones who, in their lowly understanding of God, think that when they do not understand, taste or experience him, he is far away and utterly concealed. The contrary belief would be truer. The less distinct is their understanding of him, the closer they approach him since in the words of the prophet David, 'he made darkness his hiding-place' (Psalm 18.11). Thus in drawing near him you will experience darkness because of the weakness of your eye.

You do well, then, at all times, in both adversity and prosperity, whether spiritual or temporal, to consider God as hidden, and call after him thus:

> Where have you hidden,
> Beloved, and left me moaning?

She calls him 'Beloved' to move him more to answer her prayer. When God is loved he very readily answers the requests of his lover. This he teaches through St John: 'If you abide in me, ask whatever you want and it shall be done unto you' (John 15.7). You can truthfully call God Beloved when you are wholly with him, do not allow your heart attachment to anything outside of him, and thereby ordinarily centre your mind on him. This is why Delilah asked Samson how he could say he loved her, since his spirit was not with her (Judges 16.15), and this spirit includes the mind and the affection.

Some call the Bridegroom beloved when he is not really their beloved because their heart is not wholly set on him. As a result their petition is not of much value in his sight. They do not obtain their request until they keep their spirit more continually with God through perseverance in prayer, and their heart with its affectionate love more entirely set on him. Nothing is obtained from God except by love.

# Reversed thunder
# George Herbert

*George Herbert (1593–1633) is still admired, I hope, as a poet. In his life he was admired too as a holy Anglican clergyman. This poem on prayer piles up a catalogue of sometimes strangely expressed properties of prayer. Developing the idea of a siege engine that wins heaven, Herbert even likens prayer to the spear that pierced Christ's side, not that we are the Roman soldier that wielded it but that the spear brought out flowing blood and water, traditionally types or symbols of the Eucharist and baptism, through which Christians live. (See* Ave verum corpus, *below.)*

> Prayer, the Church's banquet, angels' age,
> God's breath in man returning to his birth,
> The soul in paraphrase, heart in pilgrimage,
> The Christian's plummet, sounding heaven and earth;

Engine against the Almighty, sinner's tower,
Reversed thunder, Christ-side-piercing spear,
The six-days'-world transposing in an hour,
A kind of tune, which all things hear and fear;
Softness, and peace, and joy, and love, and bliss,
Exalted manna, gladness of the best,
Heaven in ordinary, man well drest,
The Milky Way, the bird of Paradise;
Church bells beyond the stars heard, the soul's blood,
The land of spices, something understood.

## 24

# Undefended prayer
# Mark Allen and Ruth Burrows

*Ruth Burrows (born 1924) is a Carmelite nun who has written a series of books on the spiritual life. Her postal conversation with the diplomat Mark Allen (born 1950) was published as* Letters on Prayer *in 1999.*

Very dear Ruth,

I remember a·hard but vital piece of advice you once gave to me, 'The great mistake people make ... is to abandon the times for unoccupied prayer.' That's the heart of it. You make me ask again what is this prayer and why do we find that in practice we avoid it? Why do we make this 'great mistake'?

I want to try to avoid jargon, setting up some special vocabulary for sorting out the different strands of what we mean, but by 'unoccupied prayer', you seem to be pointing at what I guess many people would really mean by 'prayer'. And why is this? Why do we make a distinction which I think you yourself would not make?

Perhaps for most lay people the usual experience of prayer is in the liturgy. And so it is primarily vocal and participatory. We go to Mass on Sundays. There will be moments of silent prayer, not least in the Eucharistic prayer around the consecration, but these are moments, and part of the mind will be very aware of what's coming next, when it will be time to stand up again. The event of going to Mass, the church setting and the fact of the holy Presence in the tabernacle and at the altar, all these work their influence. The chameleon in us is content with this background. The powerful benefits of habit are released. And we think this is different from another sort of prayer (what you mean by unoccupied prayer) because it is familiar; because we have had a lot of catechism about it; because we are not alone. That other sort which is not liturgical, is not so familiar. It is open country which we do not know, where we may fear to get lost and where, critically – and what a crisis it can be – we feel alone.

There are immediate things to be said now about faith, and the horses in your mind are probably pulling to get them out. But hold on to them for a moment because there is something else I want you to look at first. The important argument is about faith. It is the key issue, but even those who see this, do need something for the mind at first as well.

I was struck by what Hans Urs von Balthasar wrote in his book, *Prayer.* (p. 97):

Some lay people, with a view to taking a more sustained part in the liturgy of the Church, follow, to some extent, the manner of life and prayer of priests and monks, and say the daily Office either in whole or in part. But, in general, they have less understanding and spiritual freedom than those who, in the less formalised practice of contemplative prayer, allow God's life that is in them to illuminate their way. The former practice may be recommended in exceptional cases, but, for most people, it is a mistaken one.

My reaction to this was that von Balthasar was touching on the resistance most have to 'unoccupied' prayer and suggesting that lay people must not avoid this motive for resistance, but face it directly. Their response to the gift of a desire to pray should not be channelled into what could easily deteriorate into another 'activity', another form of social inclusion. They should consider the gift, reflect on it, in the silence of themselves, reaching out for the conviction that they are not alone.

I think this advice from von Balthasar could seem shocking. I wonder if you can see how powerfully magnetic for the laity inclusion in the Church can be? The good, necessary and important aspects of that pull are obvious, but there is also an undertow which I see as simply deriving from our political natures, from the fact that people are gregarious and also at root selfish, worrying about how they fit in. And that undertow seems to me to run against prayer.

In prayer and unoccupied prayer we have the chance to own up to these anxieties and to place them in the hands of Christ. We can do so without fear or inhibition. In private prayer he gives us the confidence even to find and hand over the bits we had kept back, even to accept with good humour some of the facts about ourselves which are, in this life, inescapable elements in our own make-up. My own experience is that this is the ground, the silent hard earth, in which faith first grows. 'Painfully you will get your food from it' (Genesis 3.17).

These are the reasons which, looking back, have made more and more sense to me of your advice that private, unoccupied prayer cannot be left out and why I noticed so quickly the same thought in your letter. I wonder if this makes sense to you.

With much love,

Mark

Dearest Mark,
You raise an interesting – better, an important – question. What von Balthasar writes does on the face of it seem shocking, but both

of us see that he has a point. You are in a far better position than I to verify or refute it. What we can say with certainty is that no one may predict just how God will work, what means He will use to bring each and all to himself. No two people are identical, each has her or his unique relationship with God, and God can and will guide the person, provided there is cooperation. Assuming that basic premise but leaving it aside for the moment, I think we must confront the issue in a general sort of way. At the root of it lie two inseparable, interacting, interdependent aspects of our Christian being, and they, of course, as everything else in our Christian being, have their roots in nature: solitariness and community.

Each of us is a unique, irreplaceable person, but uniquely, most truly and fully a person only in relationship to other similarly unique persons: in 'communion'. A community is something quite different from a group of people sharing common interests. Community, in the Christian sense, does not just happen, it is brought about by the Holy Spirit. The more fully each individual surrenders to this Holy Spirit, is controlled by Him, so is community really community. Works of charity, loving service, neighbourliness, all these indeed are vital, but of themselves do not create a Christian community. Our communion must be at the deepest level of being.

This must preface my attempt to answer your own shrewd observation, 'how powerfully magnetic for the laity inclusion in the Church can be . . . the undertow which I see as simply deriving from our political natures, the fact that people are gregarious and also at root selfish, worrying about how they fit in. And that undertow seems to me to run against prayer.'

Earlier you observe how easily reciting the Office and even participation in the Mass can deteriorate into another 'activity'. You are implying, if not stating baldly, that Christians in this instance are attending to one aspect of our Christian reality and neglecting the other. In so far as this is so, then community and communal prayer are impoverished. Whatever appears, there cannot be real community. 'That they may all be one; even as

130

You, Father, are in me and I in You, that they also may be one in Us' (John 17.21).

This shows the need for what we are calling 'unoccupied prayer'. What is this prayer? I shall attempt an answer, but must grope for words. Leaving aside all other occupation and, in intention, mental preoccupation, this 'me' (I shrink from saying 'I' as it seems self-assertive) 'looks at', 'comes before', 'encounters' the living God. Unoccupied prayer is equally undefended prayer: This 'me' is exposed to God, stripped of pretension, naked, refusing comforting make-believe and offering itself to be gazed at, searched out and seen in total reality by the God who, in Jesus, we know to be Absolute Love. Power, holiness, justice – whatever other attributes we impute to God are nothing but expressions of God's nature as Love. It is Love that is almighty, unutterable holiness, supremely just, and so forth. 'Fear not!' And this Love has the special quality of compassion, tender understanding and loving acceptance of us in all our sinfulness.

We can't disgust God. We might get fed up. God is never fed up, but always delights in us. So we can afford to be undefended and want this Love to enter every corner of our being because only then will everything in us be purified and transformed. When we pretend to ourselves and therefore to God, and when we are out to impress – ourselves first of all, but also God – with whatever holy sentiments, great desires or profound spirituality we think we have, God can't get at us! Again, we can arm ourselves with a plan of prayer we intend to carry through in order to make sure we don't get distracted, for that, of course, would be to fail. What is more, we absolutely dread the awareness of how spiritually inadequate we really are and our ego takes subtle precautions to ward it off. The common dodge is to avoid altogether this undefended prayer. And this is understandable enough without faith in Jesus' God.

This God longs and longs to give, not just gifts, but himself; and it is only this supreme Gift that make us utterly happy. We don't have to bribe Him with our good works or make ourselves desirable and 'worthy'. His love makes us lovely. The little story of Martha and Mary expresses the truth graphically. What Jesus is saying is that, when he enters our house, that is, when we are in direct contact with him, then it is for him to give to us, to serve and feed us, not the other way round. This, I believe, represents the reality of Christian existence: receiving God, All-Love, in Christ, letting God love us, nourish us, bring us to our total fulfilment. Well-nourished, we turn to our neighbours and share our nourishment with them. Freely we have received and freely we must give.

It is hard for us to hold onto this underlying truth. We turn it upside down, don't we? This is where I see the utmost importance of the prayer we are talking about: it expresses this truth as nothing else does. The Martha in us who wants to do things for God, wants to be the big one, the giver, must let go and childlike sit down with Mary at the feet of Jesus to receive. In doing so, her attitude will gradually change and her whole life, her serving, be purged of self-seeking and become in itself prayer. Our inmost heart must choose to remain a little one receiving its food from Jesus.

It is not easy to persevere faithfully in this solitary, defenceless prayer. We can be faced with seeming nothingness. What we have to realize is that the silence, the emptiness, if such be our experience, are filled with a love too great for human heart and mind to grasp. They are what seems, not what is.

Faith tells us that Love works and its work is Love. We have but to stay there in quiet trust, even if we suffer. This is not to say that methods are barred. Yet they must be used with a light touch and not become a screen behind which we hide our spiritual impotence. Their purpose must be to help us to maintain our undefended aloneness before our God.

It is this direct encounter of the Christian with her or his Creator and Lover that above all else creates personhood. We are not born persons in the true sense; we become persons through encounter with others, but supremely through direct encounter with God in Jesus. The two encounters are inseparable. We cannot encounter the human other in a profound way unless we are exposed to the Divine Other; but equally, unless we encounter in love the human person whom we see, we cannot encounter in love the God we cannot see (cf. I John 4.20).

Simply because we are social animals, essentially fearful, we shrink from solitary exposure. We may be using liturgical prayer as a protective screen and our tactic is effectively concealed from ourselves by liturgy's sacred character. Though in reality we are participating in something bigger than ourselves, nevertheless, we know how to do it; there are clear directives and, moreover, we are supported by others. I think von Balthasar is right to suggest a danger and you to take it up. No one can possibly judge for another or others that participation in liturgy is, in fact, an alibi. We must appraise ourselves, no one else.

I don't want to end by giving the impression that the sort of prayer we are discussing is necessarily bleak. At times it might be enrapturing. The point I want to emphasize is the unprotectedness, the naked exposure to 'the length, the breadth, the height, the depth' of reality which is the love of God that comes to us in Christ Jesus Our Lord. We are, each one, enfolded in a love so overwhelming that it escapes conception. 'As a child has rest on its mother's breast / Even so my soul' (Psalm 131.2). 'And he took them in his arms, and blessed them, laying his hands upon them' (Mark 10.16).

Our faith is not likely to be challenged at such depth when we are engaged with others in liturgical prayer. It seems to me that this unoccupied prayer is faith at its purest, refusing to stand on our own perception and casting our whole weight on the Father of Jesus. Also, it is very, very selfless: our (unfelt?) love for God overcoming self-love. Prayer is self-surrender in faith and here, I believe, we have its purest, personal expression.

With my love,

Ruth

# The sea by night
# Bede

*The Venerable Bede (673–735) was born at Wearmouth in Northumberland and spent most of his life in the monastery at Jarrow. He gives an impression of being a rounded character, and he shows the method and qualities of a true historian in his* History of the English Church and People, *written in good Latin and completed in 731. He wrote more than 40 books, including the* Life of Cuthbert *(who died when Bede was fourteen).*

Cuthbert would go forth, when others were asleep, and having spent the night in watchfulness, return home at the hour of morning prayer. Now one night, a brother of the monastery, seeing him go out alone, followed him privately to see what he should do. But he, when he left the monastery went down to the sea, which flows beneath, and going into it, until the water reached his neck and arms, spent the night in praising God.

When the dawn of day approached, he came out of the water, and, falling on his knees, began to pray again. Whilst he was doing this, two quadrupeds, called otters, came up from the sea, and, lying down before him on the sand, breathed upon his feet, and wiped them with their hair: after which, having received his blessing, they returned to their native element.

Cuthbert himself returned home in time to join in the accustomed hymns with the other brethren. The brother, who waited for him on the heights, was so terrified that he could hardly reach home; and early in the morning he came and fell at his feet, asking his pardon, for he did not doubt that Cuthbert was fully acquainted with all that had taken place. To whom Cuthbert replied, 'What is the matter, my brother? What have you done? Did you follow me to see what I was about to do? I forgive you for it on one condition – that you tell it to nobody before my death.'

# Water in itself
# George MacDonald

*George MacDonald (1824–1905) fits no pigeon-hole. From a scholarship at Aberdeen University he proceeded to the Congregationalist ministry, but his first and last charge, at Arundel, Sussex, ended after three years when the congregation complained of the lack of doctrine in his sermons. He lived frugally, though not without support from friends, on his literary pursuits after that, writing novels, children's books, poetry and fantasies, one of which,* Phantastes, *was credited by C. S. Lewis with 'baptizing his imagination'.*

*MacDonald was said to have softened the Calvinism of his upbringing, although some of his teaching sounds hard enough. Under the influence of F. D. Maurice, the Christian Socialist, he became a lay member of the Anglican Church.*

*Today he is known largely through the championship of Lewis, although at the time of his death his poetry was ranked with that of Crashaw and Vaughan. Ruskin eccentrically found evidence of the survival of religious poetry in three works: Longfellow's* Hiawatha, *Keble's* Hymns *and MacDonald's poem,* The Diary of an Old Soul.

Is oxygen-and-hydrogen the divine idea of water? Or has God put the two together only that man might separate and find them out? He allows His child to pull his toys to pieces: but were they made that he might pull them to pieces? He were a child not to be envied for whom his inglorious father would make toys to such an end! A school-examiner might see therein the best use of a toy, but not a father! Find for us what in the constitution of the two gases makes them fit and capable to be thus honoured in forming the lovely thing, and you will give us a revelation about more than water, namely about the God who made oxygen and hydrogen. There is no water in oxygen, no water in hydrogen; it comes bubbling fresh from the imagination of the living God, rushing from under the great white throne of the glacier.

The very thought of it makes one gasp with an elemental joy no metaphysician can analyse. The water itself, that dances and sings, and slakes the wonderful thirst – symbol and picture of that draught for which the woman of Samaria made her prayer to Jesus – this lovely thing itself, whose very wetness is a delight to every inch of the human body in its embrace – this live thing which, if I might, I would have running through my room, yea, babbling along my table – this water is its own self, its own truth, and is therein a truth of God. Let him who would know the truth of the Maker, become sorely athirst, and drink of the brook by the way – then lift up his heart – not at that moment to the Maker of oxygen and hydrogen, but to the Inventor and Mediator of thirst and water, that man might foresee a little of what his soul may find in God.

# 26

# Cheerful and agreeable
# James Barnard

*Richard Challoner (1691–1781), a contemporary of Alexander Pope and William Law, would seem to have lived a quiet life if this ideal day, sketched out by his first biographer, James Barnard, were all we had to go on. But he was a busy bishop in a time of upset and difficulty.*

*He had become a Catholic at the age of twelve, at the same time as his widowed mother, and went off to Douay for his schooling. He was ordained a priest and in 1730 returned to work in the London mission, it being noted that he worked much among the poor. Both the English College in Rome and Douay wanted this good and able man to head their foundations, but the Catholics of London were in great need of a bishop, and he was consecrated in 1740.*

*One does not want to exaggerate the persecutions of Catholics at that time. They were certainly barred from holding many offices, and Challoner, as a priest, was more than once prosecuted at the instigation of informers who stood to gain money. He worked calmly on, and was shaken to have to flee his house in 1780 at a great age, when the mob was busy sacking Catholic places of worship during the Gordon riots.*

*Challoner produced a large amount of useful devotional work for his flock. He also revised the Douay–Rheims translation of the Bible. He was buried at Milton, Berkshire, but his remains have now been translated to Westminster Cathedral.*

## The daily distribution of his Time; his manner of Life

What brought him to this happy state of the perfect love of God, and continual gratitude for all the benefits he has bestowed upon us, and for all the sufferings which his Son Jesus Christ endured for the love of us: was his continual and ready correspondence with the divine graces which God afforded him, to lead him on to perfection: and which he always endeavoured to cultivate and advance in his Soul by the daily practice of Meditation; and by the regularity with which he discharged all the duties of the day.

From the time of his being advanced to the Episcopal Dignity till the day of his death, this was the constant distribution of his time. Summer and winter he rose at six: and giving his first thoughts to God, and employing them in pious ejaculatory prayers till he was dressed; he then employed a whole hour in Meditation, on one or other of the pious subjects set down in his Meditations: but chiefly, as he therein recommends, insisting upon the pious affections and resolutions excited in his soul by the consideration of the proposed subject. This served as fuel to that increasing fire of divine love which burned so ardently in his breast. And this was succeeded by his immediate preparation for, and celebration of the Eucharistic Sacrifice, which he always began at eight o'clock; but on Sundays and Holy days he began it at nine o'clock, and always made it his practice on those days to preach on some Text contained in the Gospel of the day. This being finished and his usual prayers said, to return thanks to God for his having partaken of the precious body and blood of his Son in this divine Sacrament; if it was not a Fast day he took his breakfast at nine o'clock; after which he recited with great recollection, attention, and devotion, the little hours of the Divine Office, continually endeavouring to excite in his Soul, sentiments of faith, hope, love, desire, humility, contrition, and other affections, corresponding to the words made use of by the inspired writers of the Holy Scriptures, from which that Office is taken.

After which he was ready to attend to any business, concerning which any person might want to apply to him. But if no one wanted him, he then sat down to write something for the instruction and edification of his flock, or to answer Letters which he had received from different parts; still keeping his eye fixed on God, and from time to time raising his heart to him by short ejaculatory prayers, and acts of divine love. When tired with writing he would take a few turns backward and forward in his apartments: then take some pious book to read, say some prayers: or sitting in his chair contemplate on some pious subject: and then return again to his writing.

At one o'clock he used to say the evening part of the Divine Office; which finished, he used either to say some vocal prayers, or else employ himself in Meditation till Two; when, with his Chaplains, he sat down to dinner: at which time he unbent a little his mind from that close application; and was always very cheerful and agreeable: discoursing with them upon different subjects, and endeavouring to inspire them likewise with a spirit of Christian cheerfulness. If any of them had met with any mortifying or disagreeable occurrences; he would rally them, and endeavour to rouse their drooping spirits, and remind them that through many tribulations we must enter the kingdom of God: that they ought not to imagine things will always go on according to their wishes and inclinations: but to put their trust in God, and expect light, assistance and redress from him, who 'hath delivered, and doth deliver us out of great dangers'; and who, if we confide in him, 'will yet also deliver us'.

Dinner being finished, and about half an hour's more conversation; if the weather was fine, or permitted it, he would usually take one of his Chaplains with him, either to go and visit some friend, or to take a walk in the fields for the benefit of the air. But he made it his invariable practice, before ever he quitted his house, to say a short prayer, to beg that the protection and blessing of God might attend him in his excursion. His time of returning home was between five and six o'clock, when he was ready to attend those who wanted him: and from thence till supper-time, which was at nine o'clock, he employed his time in giving spiritual advice to those who applied to him, in reading, Meditation, and saying the Divine Office, and in doing what other business he had in hand.

After Supper and a little conversation, he said his prayers, examined his conscience concerning the manner in which he had discharged the duties of that day; endeavoured, by lively acts of the Theological Virtues, to put himself into the condition in which he desired to be found at the hour of his death, lest he should not live to see the morning; resigned himself into the hands of God, and then composed himself to rest under his divine protection. By this means all his actions being done for and tending to promote the greater glory of God, and the Salvation of his own and his neighbour's Souls: all his days were 'full of virtue, and of a lively hope of immortality'.

# Greeting angels
# Richard Challoner

*The advice below comes from* The Garden of the Soul, *a manual of devotions compiled by Richard Challoner that came to characterize a kind of English Catholic spirituality. It was expanded and amended into a bewildering variety of forms in subsequent decades. The edition from which this sentence is taken is that approved in 1837 by John Briggs (1788–1861), Vicar-Apostolic of the Northern District, and (from 1850) Bishop of Beverley.*

When you come into any company salute in secret the guardian
angels of the company, and beg that they would drive away the
enemy, that he may have no share in your conversation.

## 27

## Winchester lambs
## Thomas Ken

*Thomas Ken (1637–1711) lost his mother when he was four, and his father
probably when he was fourteen, at which age he was elected a scholar of
Winchester. He was an undergraduate at its sister foundation, New College,
Oxford. By 1665 he was chaplain to the Bishop of Winchester, and in his
pastoral work in the city he persuaded many unbaptized adults to undergo the
sacrament. In 1683 there was an incident when he refused to allow Nell Gwyn,
one of the king's mistresses, to be lodged in the house he had as a prebendary.
King Charles did not hold it against him, indicating in 1684 that the bishopric of
Bath and Wells should go to Ken: 'the little black fellow that refused lodging to
poor Nelly'.*

*Ken was charitable to the poor, inviting a dozen to dine with him on
Saturdays. When he gave them alms in the street he would invite them to say the
Lord's Prayer or the Creed, and finding their ignorance hopeless did what he
could to promote religous education. But he was in trouble himself under James
II, like Sancroft being tried as one of the 'Seven Bishops'. Like Sancroft too he
could not swear the oath to James's successor, William of Orange, and was
deprived of his see in 1691. He had given away most of his money and felt pained
by the way his diocese was administered by the interloping bishop.*

*The passage below comes from Ken's Manual of Prayers for Winchester
Scholars (1674); three hymns appended to it in 1695, including 'Awake my
soul', gained lasting popularity.*

As soon as ever you awake in the morning, good Philotheus, strive as much as you can, to keep all worldly thoughts out of your mind, till you have presented the first fruits of the day to God, which will be an excellent preparative to make you spend the rest of it the better; and therefore be sure to sing the morning and evening hymn in your chamber devoutly, remembering that the psalmist, upon happy experience assures you, that it is a good thing to tell of the loving kindness of the Lord early in the morning, and of His truth in the night season.

When you are ready, look on your soul as still undrest, till you have said your prayers.

Remember that God under the law ordained a lamb to be offered up to Him every morning and evening. A lamb! which is a fit emblem of youth and innocence; think then that you are to resemble this lamb, and be sure every day to offer up yourself a morning and evening sacrifice to God.

It you are a commoner, you may say your prayers in your own chamber; but if you are a child, or a chorister, then, to avoid the interruptions of the common chambers, go into the chapel, between first and second peal, in the morning, to say your morning prayers, and to say your evening prayers when you go Circum.

Now that every one may have this duty proportioned to his capacity, the best way is to distinguish two degrees of young Christians in this college, namely, those that are of an age capable of receiving the holy sacrament, and those that are not; and in one of these two degrees you are to rank yourself.

*Morning prayer*
Glory be to Thee, O Lord God, for all the blessings I daily receive from Thee, and for Thy particular preservation, and refreshment of me, this night past.

O Lord, have mercy upon me, and forgive whatsoever Thou hast seen amiss in me this night; and for the time to come give me grace to fly all youthful lusts, and to remember Thee, my Creator, in the days of my youth.

141

Shower down Thy graces, and blessings on me, and on my relations (on my father and mother, on my brethren and sisters) on all my friends, on all my governors in this place, and on all my fellow-scholars, and give Thy angels charge over us, to protect us all from sin and danger.

Lord, bless me in my learning this day, that I may every day grow more fit for Thy service: O pardon my failings, and do more for me than I can ask, or think, for the merits of Jesus my Saviour, in whose holy words I sum up all my wants. Our Father, which art in heaven, etc.

*Evening prayer*
Glory be to Thee, O Lord God, for all the blessings I daily receive from Thee, and for Thy particular preservation of me this day.

O Lord, have mercy upon me, and forgive whatsoever Thou hast seen amiss in me this day past; and for the time to come give me grace to fly all youthful lusts, and to remember Thee my Creator in the days of my youth.

Lord, receive me and all my relations, and all that belong to this college, into Thy gracious protection this night, and send me such seasonable rest, that I may rise the next morning, more fit for Thy service.

Lord, hear my prayers, and pardon my failings, for the merits of my blessed Saviour, in whose holy words I sum up all my wants. Our Father, which art in heaven, etc.

This, good Philotheus, is the lowest degree of duty, and it should be your daily endeavour to improve in your devotion, as well as in your learning.

*Directions for reading Holy Scripture*
When you have said your morning prayer, good Philotheus, you may then go cheerfully to your study, and rely upon the divine goodness for a blessing.

But first, if you have time, I advise you to read before second peal, some short psalm, or piece of a chapter out of the gospel, or historical books, because they are the most easy to be understood; remembering the example of young Timothy, who was bred up to know the Scripture from a child.

But if you want time on ordinary days to read the Scripture, be sure to read somewhat of it on Sundays and holidays, and consider, that you have it daily read to you in the hall before dinner and supper, and at night when you are just going to bed, that you may close the day with holy thoughts; and if you hearken diligently to it when it is read, you do in effect read it yourself.

Now to make your reading the more profitable to you, begin. with one or more of these ejaculations:

Wherewithal, Lord, shall a young man cleanse his way? Even by ruling himself after Thy words.

Lord, open my eyes, that I may see the wonderful things of Thy law.

O heavenly Father! I humbly beg Thy Holy Spirit so to help me at this time to read, and understand, and to remember and practise Thy word, that it may make me wise to salvation.

When you are thus prepared, good Philotheus, then begin to read, and consider, that it is God's most holy word you read; and that all the while you are reading, God is speaking to you, and therefore read with attention and humility, and endeavour, as much as you can to suit your affections to the subject you read.

For instance, if you read any of God's commands, they should excite in you a zeal to keep them.

If you read any of God's threatenings against sinners, or His judgements on them, they should excite in you a fear to provoke Him.

When you read any of His gracious promises, they should encourage and quicken your obedience.

When you read any of God's mercies, they should excite you to thanksgiving.

143

When you read any great mystery recorded in holy writ, you are to prostrate your reason to divine revelation.

And to this purpose, in the midst of your reading, say:

Lord, give me grace to obey this command; *or,*

Lord, deliver me from this sin: or, this judgement; *or,*

Lord, I rely on this good promise; *or,*

Glory be to Thee, O Lord, for this mercy; *or,*

Lord, I believe and adore this mystery.

Say any of these, according as best agrees with the subject you read, and when you have read as much as conveniently you can, conclude with one of these ejaculations:

Blessed be Thou, O Lord, O teach me Thy statutes.

Lord, make Thy word a lantern unto my feet, and a light unto my paths.

Lord, make Thy word my delight and my counsellor.

# God be in my head

*From* The Sarum Primer, *1527.*

> God be in my head
> And in my understanding.
> God be in my eyes
> And in my looking.
> God be in my mouth
> And in my speaking.
> God be in my heart
> And in my thinking.
> God be at my end
> And my departing.

# 28

## Savaged by wild boars
## *The Cloud of Unknowing*

*The* Cloud of Unknowing *was written by an unknown hand in the last quarter of the fourteenth century, a century that produced three English writers profoundly committed to contemplative prayer: Julian of Norwich, Walter Hilton and Richard Rolle.*

*The author of* The Cloud of Unknowing *was strongly influenced by another unknown author of eight centuries earlier, whose writings circulated under the name of Denis or Dionysius the Areopagite. The general misapprehension that the author was the Athenian mentioned in the New Testament gave his work much greater status than it would have enjoyed otherwise, but the fact remained that its doctrine of the* via negativa *influenced spiritual writers in all succeeding generations. This idea was that God cannot be accurately described by any of the concepts that we possess as limited creatures. Only by faith exercised in prayer can he make himself known by presence in the soul.*

*Denis's theory does not swamp the practical treatise by the author of* The Cloud of Unknowing, *who discusses here what to do about the remains of sin in the soul seeking God.*

### *Chapter 31* **How a person should react at the beginning of this work against all thoughts and stirrings of sin.**
When you feel that you have done what you can lawfully to amend yourself, according to the precepts of the Holy Church, then you should set yourself to work energetically in a new work. But then, if something particular that you had done before should oppress your mind, coming between you and your God, or any new thoughts, or the stirring of any sin either, you should resolutely rise above them with a fervent stirring of love, and tread them down under your

feet. Try to cover them with a thick cloud of forgetting, as though they never had been done in this life by you, or by any one else. And if they rise up often, put them down often: in short, as often as they rise up, put them down. If you think that the effort is great, then look for ways and means and contrive personal techniques of driving them away from your soul. These techniques are better learned from God through our own experience than from any person on earth.

### Chapter 32 Of two spiritual techniques that are helpful to a spiritual beginner in the work that is the subject of this book.

Nevertheless I can tell you something of my own ideas about such techniques. Try them, or do better if you can.

Do what you can to behave as though you did not feel that such thoughts interfered so intrusively between you and your God. Try to look, as it were, over their shoulders, looking for something else. That something else is God, enclosed in a cloud of unknowing. If you do this, I am sure that within a short time you will find your hard labours easing. I am sure that if this tactic is tried out in your mind properly, it will bring nothing else but a longing for God, a desire to feel him and to see him, if one could, here. Such a desire is charity; and it always deserves to be accommodated.

Another technique that you could try if you wanted is, when you feel that you cannot put these thoughts aside at all, sink beneath them as if you were a defeated coward in battle, and realize that it is nothing but foolishness to struggle any longer against them – but just surrender to God while still in the hands of your enemies. You may then feel as though you were overcome for ever. Take note of this technique, please; for I think that in trying it you will melt everything in water. And I am sure that if this tactic is tried out in your mind properly, it will bring nothing else but a true realization and appreciation of yourself as you are, a wretch and a dirty thing perhaps, and far worse than nothing at all. Realizing and appreciating this is humility. This humility brings almighty God himself down to take revenge on your enemies and to take you up and lovingly dry the eyes of your spirit, as a father does if his child is almost savaged by wild boars.

**Chapter 33** **In this work a soul is cleansed both of its personal sins and of the pain of them. Yet in this life there is no complete rest.**

I won't discuss any more techniques at this stage; for if you have grace to experience such things, I am sure that you will be better able to teach me than I can you. For, although things are as I have explained, yet I think I am far from having accomplished all this myself. So please help me, and take action on your own behalf and on mine too.

Carry on, and work hard for a while, please, and humbly put up with the pain if you can't achieve these habits soon. For it is your purgatory. Then when your pain has all passed, and your God-given habits are confirmed by practice, then there seems no doubt to me that you are cleansed not only from sin, but also from the pain of sin. I mean from the pain of your former personal sins – not from the penalty of Original Sin. For that penalty will stay with you until the day you die, no matter how you try. Nevertheless it will not trouble you very much compared with the pain of your personal sins; and despite that you will still have hard work. For from Original Sin every day spring fresh stirrings of sin. These have to be cut away every day. Be ready to cut them away with the sharp double-edged sword of discretion. By its help you will be able to learn that there is no true security, and no true rest in this life.

Nevertheless, you should not turn back because of that, nor should you be overmuch afraid of failing. For if you have the grace to destroy the pain of your former personal sins in the way I have mentioned, or by a better technique if you know of one, then rest assured the penalties of Original Sin and fresh stirrings of sin in the future will hardly be able to trouble you.

# Confidence in God
## George Herbert

*In a more difficult poem than his better-known sonnet on prayer, Herbert finds himself questioning whether he was right to take orders, and counters the doubt by casting himself on God's kind providence.*

*By 'licorous' he might as easily mean 'greedy' as 'lecherous'. By 'Man and the present fit; if he provide, | He breaks the square', he means that to 'provide' or 'look forward' is to break the 'square' or agreement with God, that the future is his to look after. I think that the phrase later on, 'draw the bottome out an end', means 'pull a thread from the spool', that is, unroll a whole ball of grief.*

**The discharge**

> Busie enquiring heart, what wouldst thou know?
>> Why dost thou prie,
> And turn, and leer, and with a licorous eye
>> Look high and low,
>> And in thy lookings stretch and grow?

> Hast thou not made thy counts and summ'd up all?
>> Did not thy heart
> Give up the whole and with the whole depart?
>> Let what will fall,
>> That which is past who can recall?

> Thy life is God's, thy time to come is gone,
>> And is his right.
> He is thy night at noon, he is at night
>> Thy noon alone.
>> The crop is his, for he hath sown.

> And well it was for thee, when this befell,
>> That God did make

Thy businesse his, and in thy life partake;
    For thou canst tell,
  If it be his once, all is well.

Only the present is thy part and fee.
    And happy thou
If, though thou didst not beat thy future brow,
    Thou couldst well see
  What present things requir'd of thee.

They ask enough. Why shouldst thou further go?
    Raise not the mudde
Of future depths, but drink the cleare and good.
    Dig not for woe
  In times to come, for it will grow.

Man and the present fit; if he provide,
    He breaks the square.
This houre is mine; if for the next I care,
    I grow too wide,
  And do encroach upon death's side.

For death each houre environs and surrounds.
    He that would know
And care for future chances, cannot go
    Unto those grounds
  But through a Church-yard which them bounds.

Things present shrink and die. But they that spend
    Their thoughts and sense
On future grief, do not remove it thence,
    But it extend,
  And draw the bottome out an end.

God chains the dog till night. Wilt loose the chain,

149

And wake thy sorrow?
Wilt thou forestall it, and now grieve tomorrow,
And then again
Grieve over freshly all thy pain?

Either grief will not come, or if it must,
Do not forecast.
And while it cometh it is almost past.
Away distrust!
My God hath promis'd, he is just.

# 29

# Troubles from the past
# Teresa of Avila

*Teresa of Avila (1515–82) was forty when she felt moved to change her own way of life to give contemplative prayer the utmost importance. She had already been a nun for twenty years but now set about founding a string of new convents that could observe a reformed version of the vocation of the Carmelite order. As a woman in the rather suffocating atmosphere of Spain under Philip II she found this no easy task, though she proceeded with calm determination and a sense of humour.*

*Having written the story of her life, at the request of her confessor, in 1565, she found that he would not permit the manuscript to be read by the nuns of her new foundation of St Joseph's. So, with their encouragement, she turned the next year to the task of writing a book for them about the spiritual life, in particular prayer. This book became known as* The Way of Perfection.

*The attitude to mental prayer that Teresa had to counter she characterizes in this way: 'It's not for women, for they will fall prey to delusions. It is better for them to stick to their sewing – they have no need for these technicalities.*

*The Our Father and the Hail Mary will suffice.' She scolds her critics, saying: 'Well, how is it, you Christians, that you call mental prayer unnecessary? Do you understand it yourselves? Really, I do not think you do, for you want us all to be misled. You do not know what mental prayer is or how vocal prayers should be said, or what contemplation is.'*

*In* The Way of Perfection, *Teresa not only explains how to persevere in prayer but also gives heart to those beset by apparent difficulties, such as the confused ideas of their own sinfulness that she addresses here.*

My daughters, beware of certain kinds of humility sent by the devil which give us great disquiet about the gravity of our past sins. There are many ways in which he can afflict us, even to making us give up Communion and private prayer, because the devil suggests to us that we are not worthy. When such people approach the Blessed Sacrament, they spend the time during which they ought to be receiving grace in wondering whether they are properly prepared or not. Things get so bad that a soul can be made to believe that, because of what it is, it has been forsaken by God – it almost doubts his mercy. Everything such a person does appears to her to be dangerous, and all the service she renders, however good it may be, seems to her fruitless. She loses confidence and sits idle, with her hands in her lap, because she thinks she cannot do anything well, and that what is good in others is wrong in herself.

Pay great attention, daughters, to the point which I am going to make now, because sometimes thinking yourselves so wicked may be humility and virtue and at other times a very great temptation. I know this because I have experienced it. Humility, however deep it be, does not disquiet or trouble or disturb the soul; it is accompanied by peace, joy and tranquillity. Although we can see clearly that we deserve to be in hell, on realizing how wicked we are, and we are distressed by our sinfulness, and rightly think that everyone should hate us, yet, if our humility is true, this distress is accompanied by an interior peace and joy which we should not like to be without. Far from disturbing or afflicting the soul, it enlarges it and makes it fit to serve God more. The other kind of distress only

151

disturbs and afflicts the mind and troubles the soul, and is very grievous. I think the devil wants us to think that we are humble, and, if he can, to lead us to distrust God.

When you find yourselves in this state, stop thinking of your own wretchedness, so far as you can, and turn your thoughts to God's mercy and his love and how he has suffered for us. If your state of mind is the result of temptation, you will not be able even to do this, for it will not let you quiet your thoughts or to fix them on anything but will only weary you the more. It will be a great thing to recognize this as a temptation.

This can happen when we undertake excessive penance in order to make ourselves believe that, because of what we perform, we are more penitent than others. If we conceal our penance from our confessor or superior, or if we are told to give them up and do not obey, that is a clear case of temptation. Always try to obey, however much it hurts you to do so, for that is the greatest possible perfection.

There is another very dangerous kind of temptation: a feeling of complacency caused by the belief that we shall never again return to our past faults and to worldly pleasures. 'I know all about these things now', we say, 'and I realize that they all come to an end and I get more pleasure from the things of God.' If this temptation comes to beginners it is very dangerous, because, having this sense of complacency, they think nothing of running once more into occasions of sin. They soon trip over these – and then God preserve them from falling back farther than before! The devil, seeing that these souls may do him harm and be of great help to others, does all in his power to prevent them from rising again. So, however many consolations and pledges of love the Lord may give you, you must never be so complacent that you stop being afraid of falling again; and you must keep yourselves from occasions of sin.

Do all you can to discuss these favours and consolations with someone who can enlighten you; have no secrets from him. However sublime your contemplation, take great care to begin and to end every period of prayer with self-examination. If these favours come from God, you will do this more frequently, without either taking or needing any advice from me, for such favours bring humility with them and always leave us with more light by which we may see how small we are. I won't say any more now, for you will find many books which give advice of this kind. I have said these things because I have had experience of the matter and have sometimes found myself in difficulties of this nature. Nothing that can be said about it, however, will give us complete security.

What, then, Eternal Father, can we do but flee to you and beg you not to allow these enemies of ours to lead us into temptation? If attacks are made upon us openly, we shall easily be freed from them, with your help. But how can we master these treacherous assaults, my God? We need at all times to pray for your help. Teach us, Lord, some way of recognizing them and guarding against them. You know that few walk along this road already, and if so many fears are to beset them, there will be far fewer.

# At the end of the day
# John Henry Newman

*J. H. Newman (1801–90) acquired a knowledge of the early Fathers of the Church that was highly unusual at the beginning of the nineteenth century. Combined with his own idealism, feeling and logical strength, this knowledge informed the developments of his long life. The prayer here was translated by Newman in 1834, when he was still an Anglican, from St Gregory of Nazianzus (329–89), a holy ascetic of Cappadocia to whom Jerome owed much.*

**An evening prayer**
> O holiest Truth! How have I lied to Thee!
> I vow'd this day Thy festival should be:
>    But I am dim ere night.
> Surely I made my prayer, and I did deem
> That I could keep in me Thy morning beam,
>    Immaculate and bright.

But my foot slipp'd; and as I lay, he came,
My gloomy foe, and robb'd me of heaven's flame.
Help Thou my darkness, Lord, till I am light.


# 30

## Half-hearted hell
## Augustine Baker

*Augustine Baker (1575–1641) was born in Abergavenny and christened
David. He went to Oxford and was admitted to the Inner Temple as a lawyer
in 1596. By then he was so far from following religion that at his brother's
death-bed he could not even remember the words of the Lord's Prayer.*

*He turned to God in 1600 after a close deliverance from drowning in a river
in raging flood. He was reconciled to the Catholic Church in 1603 and became
a Benedictine monk in 1605, taking the name Augustine. It was impossible for
reasons of safety to live a monastic life in Wales or England at that time, and
though Baker undertook historical research in London, he found himself in
1624 chaplain to a new foundation of English nuns at Cambrai (its descendant
is Stanbrook Abbey). For them he collected books on the interior life and
compiled one of his own, edited and published in 1657 by Serenus Cressy under
the title* Sancta Sophia. *It remains a classic of the spiritual life.*

*Poor Baker became embroiled in other people's controversies about how
active a Benedictine monk should be, and he himself showed a startling lack of
tact in pressing his views. Dom David Knowles in the 1960s criticized Baker
for concentrating on prayer alone 'as an effort or activity distinguished from
other virtues or activities of the Christian life'. But Baker obediently followed
orders in 1638 to return as a missioner to England, where he frequently
changed his lodgings near the inns of Court to escape the attentions of
government informers. Three years later he died of a fever and was buried in
the churchyard of St Andrew's Holborn.*

*His remarks here on the pain and danger of tepidity apply to lay people as far as they have undertaken a life of prayer.*

A pressing motive to a courageous resolution of prosecuting internal ways once begun, and a strong proof of the extreme necessity thereof, is the consideration of the extreme danger and miseries unexpressible of a negligent and tepid life, whether in religion or in the world; the which not only renders perfection impossible to be attained, but endangers the very root of essential sanctity and all pretension to eternal happiness.

Tepidity is a bitter poisonous root fixed in the minds of negligent Christians, who though out of a servile fear they abstain from an habitual practice of acknowledged mortal actual sins, and therefore (groundlessly enough) think themselves secure from the danger of hell, yet they perform their external necessary obligations to God and their brethren sleepily and heartlessly, without any true affection, contenting themselves with the things however outwardly done; yea, perhaps knowing no perfection beyond this; but in the mean time remain full of self-love, inward pride, sensual desires, aversion from internal conversation with God, etc. And the ground and cause of this pernicious tepidity is want of affection and esteem of spiritual things, and a voluntary affection to venial sins (not as they are sins, but as the objects of them are easeful or delightful to nature), joined with a wilfulness not to avoid the occasions of them, nor to do any more in God's service than what themselves judge to be necessary for the escaping of hell.

Such persons, if they live in religion, must needs pass very uncomfortable and discontented lives, having excluded themselves from the vain entertainments and pleasures of the world, and yet retaining a strong affection to them in their hearts, with an incapacity of enjoying them. They must undergo all obligations, austerities and crosses incident to a religious state without comfort, but only in having despatched them, with very little benefit to their souls, and with extreme wearisomeness and unwillingness. Now, what a resemblance to hell hath such a life, where there is an

155

impossibility freely to enjoy what the soul principally desires, and where she is forced continually to do and suffer such things as are extremely contrary to her inclinations!

Whereas, if souls would courageously at once give themselves wholly to God, and with a discreet fervour combat against corrupt nature, pursuing their internal exercises, they would find that all things would cooperate, not only to their eternal good, but even to their present contentment and joy. They would find pleasure even in their greatest mortifications and crosses, by considering the love with which God sends them, and the great benefit that their spirit reaps by them. What contentment can be greater to any soul than to become a true inward friend of God, chained unto Him with a love, the like whereto never was between any mortal creatures to know and even feel that she belongs to God, and that God is continually watchful over her, and careful of her salvation? None of which comforts tepid souls can hope to taste; but, on the contrary, are not only continually tortured with present discontents, but much more with a fear and horror, considering their doubtfulness about their future state ...

For when such souls approach near unto death, they will then too late consider that for want of diligent prayer there may be, yea, assuredly are in them, a world of inordinations, impurities and defects undiscovered by them, and therefore can neither be acknowledged nor bewailed; so that they cannot have any assurance of the state and inclinations of their souls; besides, they know themselves to have been guilty of a life spent in an uninterrupted ingratitude to God, who gave them light to see the ways to perfection which their profession obliged them to walk in, and yet wilfully they neglected to make use of such light, or to make progress in those ways, etc. (and this is all aggravation of guilt beyond the former); they are conscious likewise of an unexcusable and long continued unfaithfulness, never almost complying with the divine inspirations which daily urged them to put themselves resolutely into that only secure way of an internal life, nor ever vigorously resisting the sins and imperfections which they did discover in themselves, etc. Such sad thoughts as these pressing (as usually they do) one upon another near the approaches of death, what grievous apprehensions, what terrible uncertainties must they needs cause in tepid souls, then most sensible of dangers and fears! so that their lives will be full of anguish and continual remorse, and their deaths very uncomfortable.

Lastly, to all these miseries of a tepid life, this also may be added as an increase of the guilt, and consequently an aggravation of the dangerous state of souls infected with that poison, which is, that they do not only themselves most ungratefully withdraw their own affections from God and divine things, but by their ill example, by misspending the time in vain extroverted conversations, by discountenancing those that are fervourous in internal ways, etc., they infect their companions, and so treacherously defraud Almighty God of the affections of others also. So that a tepid religious person, though given to no enormous excesses, is oft more harmful in a community than as open, scandalous liver; because none that hath any care of himself but will beware of such an one as this latter is; whereas a tepid soul unperceivably instils into others the poisonous infection wherewith herself is tainted.

From the grounds and considerations here mentioned, it doth appear how necessary it is for a devout soul, both in the beginning and pursuance of a contemplative life, to excite and fortify her courageous resolution not to be daunted by discouragements either from within or without, but at what price soever, and with what labours and sufferings soever, with fervour to persevere in the exercises and duties belonging thereto, accounting tepidity and spiritual sloth as the very bane of her whole design, the which, if it be yielded unto, though but a little, it will gather more force, and at last grow irresistible.

But withal she is to be advised that such her courage and fervour must be exercised, not impetuously out of passion, or such impulses as a fit of sensible devotees will sometimes produce in her; but this fervour and resolution must chiefly be seated in the superior will, and regulated by spiritual discretion, according to her present forces, both natural and supernatural, and the measure of grace bestowed on her, and no further; for there may be as much harm by outrunning grace, as by neglecting to correspond unto it. Hence, it oft comes to pass that many well-minded souls, being either pushed forward by an indiscreet passionate zeal or advised by unexperienced directors to undertake unnecessarily and voluntarily either rigorous mortifications or excessive tasks of devotions, and wanting strength to continue them, have become able to do nothing at all; so that affecting too hastily to attain unto perfection sooner than God did enable them thereto, they so overburden themselves that they are forced to give over quite all tendence to it. Therefore we must be contented to proceed in such a pace as may be lasting, and that will suffice.

## A warming wasp
## Edward Taylor

*Edward Taylor (1642–1729) was a Calvinist minister in what was then the frontier town of Westfield in Massachusetts. The hardness of Calvinism comes out in some of his poetical addresses to God:*

> *Such as will not with thy rule Comply*
> *Thou with thy iron Sceptre down will smite.*
> *This Power will raise the dead, and judge all too.*
> *His own will Crown with Life. To hell foes Throw.*

*But since the fore-ordaining of God counts every hair, signs of God are to be discerned in all creation, as with the chilled wasp.*

*Taylor was born quite close to George Fox, near Sketchley, Leicestershire, a generation later. With the Act of Uniformity of 1662 dissenting ministers lost their chance to take up establishment positions, and in 1668 Taylor sailed for America. His ministry began after three years at Harvard. His first wife bore eight children, five of whom died in infancy, upon which Taylor reflected:*

> *But oh! The tortures, Vomit, screechings, groans,*
> *And six-week Fever would pierce hearts like stones.*

*After his first wife's death he married again, and had six more children.*

*In the first decade of Taylor's ministry, attacks by Indians almost succeeded in forcing the settlers out. But by the end of his life, the people of Westfield had built a fine new meeting house, which he refused to move to.*

*The bulk of his poetry is made up of 'Preparatory Meditations before my Approach to the Lord's Supper'. He forbade the publication of his poetry in his lifetime or by his descendants. Manuscripts remained in Yale University Library, and the first selection from his work did not appear in print until 1937.*

### Upon a Wasp Chil'd with Cold

The Bare that breaths the Northern blast
Did numb, Torpedo like, a Wasp
Whose stiffend limbs encrampt, lay bathing
In Sol's warm breath and shine as saving,
Which with her hands she chafes and stands
Rubbing her Legs, Shanks, Thighs, and hands.
Her petty toes, and fingers ends
Nipt with this breath, she out extends
Unto the Sun, in greate desire
To warm her digits at that fire.
Doth hold her Temples in this state
Where pulse doth beate, and head doth ake.
Doth turn, and stretch her body small,
Doth Comb her velvet Capitall.
As if her little brain pan were
A Volume of Choice precepts cleare.
As if her satin jacket hot
Contained Apothecaries Shop
Of Nature's recepts, that prevails
To remedy all her sad ailes,
As if her velvet helmet high
Did turret rationality.
She fans her wing up to the Winde
As if her Pettycoate were lin'de,

159

With reasons fleece, and hoises sails.
And humming flies in thankfull gails
Unto her dun Curld palace Hall
Her warm thanks offering for all.

Lord cleare my misted sight that I
May hence view thy Divinity.
Some sparkes whereof thou up dust hasp
Within this little downy Wasp
In whose small Corporation we
A school and a schoolmaster see
Where we may learn, and easily finde
A nimble Spirit bravely minde
Her worke in e'ry limb: and lace
It up neate with a vitall grace,
Acting each part though ne'er so small
Here of this Fustian animall.
Till I enravisht Climb into
The Godhead on this Lather doe.
Where all my pipes inspir'de upraise
An Heavenly musick furrd with praise.

# Kate seems kinder
# Martin Luther

*Martin Luther (1483–1535) changed the face of Christianity by what he did as well as what he wrote, which was voluminous. His* Table Talk *catches him in informal mood, but in this example still turning over the predominant concern of his life: his relations with Jesus Christ as Saviour. The translation is by the essayist William Hazlitt (1778–1830).*

I expect more goodness from Kate my wife, from Philip Melancthon, and from other friends, than from my sweet and blessed Saviour Christ Jesus; and yet I know for certain, that neither she nor any other person on earth, will or can suffer that for me which he has suffered; why then should I be afraid of him! This my foolish weakness grieves me very much. We plainly see in the gospel, how mild and gentle he showed himself towards his disciples; how kindly he passed over their weakness, their presumption, yea, their foolishness. He checked their unbelief, and in all gentleness admonished them. Moreover, the Scripture, which is most sure, says: 'Well are all they that put their trust in him.'

Fie on our unbelieving hearts, that we should be afraid of this man, who is more loving, friendly, gentle and compassionate towards us than are our kindred, our brethren and sisters; yea, than parents themselves are towards their own children.

He that has such temptations, let him be assured, it is not Christ, but the envious devil that affrights, wounds, and would destroy him; for Christ comforts, heals and revives.

# 32

# Unbloody sacrifice
# Anthony Sparrow

*Anthony Sparrow (1612–85) wrote* A Rationale upon the Book of Common Prayer *(1655) at a time when he had been ejected as rector of his parish for using the Book of Common Prayer under the Commonwealth. His commentary, like those of Robert Nelson or Thomas Comber, sold well for many years.*

*Sparrow, who eventually became Bishop of Norwich, wrote in the tradition of the Caroline divines who sought to preserve a connection of the Church of England with the teachings of the ancient Fathers of the Church. His treatment in the* Rationale *of the word 'priest' encapsulates his understanding of the Eucharist in Anglican practice.*

The Greek and Latin Words, which we translate *Priest*, are derived from Words which signify Holy; and so the Word *Priest*, according to the Etymology, signifies him whose mere Charge and Function is about holy Things. And therefore seems to be a most proper Word for him who is set apart to the holy publick Service and Worship of God: Especially when he is in the actual Ministration of holy Things. Wherefore in the Rubrics which direct him in his Ministration of these holy publick Services, the Word *Priest* is most commonly used, both by this Church and all the primitive Churches, Greek and Latin, as far as I can find: And I believe it can scarce be found that in any of the old Greek and Latin Liturgies, the Word *Presbyter* was used in the Rubrics that direct the Order of Service; but in the Greek, *hiereus*, and in the Latin, *Sacerdos*, which we in English translate *Priest*, which I suppose to be done upon this Ground, that this Word *Priest* is the most proper for him that ministers, in the Time of his Ministration.

If it is to be objected that, according to the usual Acceptation of the Word, it signifies him that offers up a Sacrifice, and therefore cannot be allowed to a Minister of the Gospel, who hath no Sacrifice to offer: It is answered; That the Ministers of the Gospel have Sacrifices to offer (St Peter, first Epist, chap. ii) 'Ye are built up a spiritual House, an holy Priesthood to offer up spiritual Sacrifices of prayer, Praises, Thanksgivings', etc. In Respect of these, the Ministers of the Gospel may be safely in a metaphorical Sense called Priests; and in a more eminent manner than other Christians are; because they are taken from among Men, to offer up their Sacrifices for others. But besides these Spiritual Sacrifices mentioned, the Ministers of the Gospel have another Sacrifice to offer, viz. The unbloody Sacrifice, as it was anciently called, the commemorative Sacrifice of the Death of Christ; which does as really and truly shew forth the Death of Christ as those Sacrifices under the Law did foreshew it; and in Respect of this Sacrifice of the Eucharist, the Antients have usually called those that offer it up *Priests*. And if Melchisedeck was called a *Priest* (as he is often by St Paul to the Hebrews) who yet had no other Offering or Sacrifice, that we read of, but that of Bread and Wine – (Genesis 14) 'He brought forth Bread and Wine and' (or 'for', the Hebrew Word bears both) 'he was a Priest'; that is, this Act of his was an Act of Priesthood, for so must it be referred: 'he brought forth Bread and Wine, for he was a Priest' and not thus, 'and he was a Priest, and blessed Abraham'; for both in the Hebrew and Greek, there is a full Point after these Words, 'and', or, 'for he was a Priest'.

If, I say, Melchisedeck be frequently and truly called a *Priest*, who had no other Offering that we read of but Bread and Wine; why may not they, whose Office is to bless the People, as Melchisedeck did, and besides that, to offer that holy Bread and Wine, the Body and Blood of Christ, of which his Bread and Wine at the most was but a Type, be as truly, and without Offence, called *Priests* also?

# Ave verum corpus

*This short Eucharistic hymn dates from the fourteenth century.*

Ave verum Corpus natum
De Maria Virgine:
Vere passum, immolatum
In cruce pro homine:
Cuius latus perforatum
Unda fluxit et sanguine:
Esto nobis praegustatum
Mortis in examine.

[Hail, true Body born of the Virgin Mary, you who have truly suffered and been sacrificed on the cross for man. You from whose pierced side water and blood flowed, in the ordeal test of death be for us a foretaste of heaven.]

## 33

# Lay aside hat and sword
# John Gother

*John Gother (died 1704) was born probably at some time during the Commonwealth years. His parents were Presbyterians, but he became a Roman Catholic and went to Lisbon in 1668 to study for the priesthood there at the English College. He returned to England in 1682 and worked as a pastor until his death. He was to instruct and receive into the Catholic Church Richard Challoner, the dominating personality among English Catholics in the eighteenth century. Gother himself produced many volumes of instruction and devotion, in vigorous and readable style. John Dryden liked to say that Gother was the only person 'besides himself' who knew how to write the English language.*

*In his introduction to his book* Afternoon Instructions for Sundays, *from which the passage below is taken, Gother remarks: 'If there are sometimes some severe expressions, the perverseness of a corrupt world, obstinate in iniquity, must be my apology; it lies charmed in a dead sleep; and if nothing less than thunder be necessary to awaken it, what help would there be in a soft whisper and a gentle admonition?' But he knew when to be gentle at need, reconciling sinners, and visiting the poor, mothers bereaved in childbirth, the sick, the dying, prisoners and those condemned to death.*

*Here, he considers preparation for Holy Communion, then a much rarer practice than now, though to be undertaken annually at least.*

## Palm Sunday

Having discoursed, last Sunday, of preparations necessary for approaching to the blessed Sacrament, we are now to go and finish that subject, according to the exigency of the present time. When a Christian therefore, has composed his mind in some tolerable degree of peace, by true repentance, and done this so seasonably that he has now time wholly to apply himself in preparing for the holy communion, he is to make this preparation the general subject of his endeavours and thoughts.

*First*, On the evening before, when he lies down to sleep, he is to entertain his heart with the wonders of God's goodness to which he is invited, and let these shut out all other thoughts. If he awakes in the night, the same considerations ought to stand ready, waiting for the first admittance. In the morning again, the same are to be recalled, and a certain joy, mixt with fear, ought to possess his mind, upon the apprehension of that inestimable, and yet dreadful favour, which he is to receive from God that day. Having thus turned his heart towards God, and afterwards dealing all unnecessary business and conversation, which cannot but bring distraction with them, with the best convenience he is to go to his prayers; and having adored God in union with all the blessed in Heaven, and begged his assistance in the great work he has to do,

165

he begins those prayers which are composed for this purpose as a preparation for the holy communion; and no solicitude of finishing any usual task of other prayers ought to put these by, but these are to take place of all. They are to be said with the best attention and greatest fervour of spirit; for that a bare and cold recital of them can be no help, but is going so far out of the way.

But the best part of the preparation is not to be had from books, except only by way of direction or hint; but in the interior exercise of the heart, taken up with such considerations as the present circumstances suggest, which may be something after this method.

*First*, He considers the infinite majesty and holiness of God, in whose sight the angels are not pure, and before whom the pillars of heaven tremble.

*2ndly*, He gives a general glance at his own unworthiness contracted by his infinite neglects, by his ingratitude, by the number and foulness of his sins.

*3rdly*, Upon this he humbles himself, confessing that he deserves to be forever banished from the sight of God, and stands surprised at his own presumption in waiting to receive his Lord.

*4thly*, Thus considering God and himself, he fears, and cannot but tremble at the thought of so unworthy a sinner making so near an approach to God; he thinks it is more fitting he should hide himself, or like Jonah fly from before the face of God.

*5thly*, He calls to mind the infinite goodness and mercies of his God; how much he has done, how much he has suffered for sinners; with what solicitude he has sought them, with what love he invites them to him.

*6thly*, Upon this prospect he recovers his sinking spirits, and raises a confidence in God; resting with an entire hope in him, that he, who has so abounded in goodness as to provide this banquet for the help and comfort of repenting sinners, and called them to it, will pardon his presumption, and mercifully receive him, who in all humility obeys his call, and offers himself a guest to his table.

*7thly*, He falls down and adores this infinite goodness which he sees in God; invites all the blessed above to adore with him and bless his holy name and protests that he has no confidence in himself, but only the goodness of God.

*8thly*, He considers the design of God's goodness in this institution of mercy; and hence begins to hope that since God has ordained it, he shall from this food of life receive a new life; that being miserable and weak, he shall here recover strength; that he shall be raised above his former self and by the help of divine grace be prepared against all assaults and for a more faithful discharge of all duties.

*9thly*, With this hope he puts himself forward, and professes to God that he comes to him as one infirm and sick to his physician; as an undutiful child to the bowels of a tender father; as an unhappy wanderer to a faithful guide; as one in distress to a powerful protector and friend; as one perishing through hunger to a plentiful table; finally as a wretched sinner to his merciful God. And then begs that God would graciously look upon him, and dispense his blessings to him according to his wants.

*Lastly*, He again humbles himself at the consideration of the little he has done to prepare himself, begs pardon for all neglects and manifests this his desire at least that in whatever manner he comes short of what he ought to do, his most earnest desire is, that all were so duly prepared within him, that his breast might become a worthy mansion for his Lord.

In this manner the good Christian endeavours to prepare his soul, that when his Lord comes, he may find it adorned, and a welcome habitation in it. Those who can but apprehend how great an advantage there is in such a preparation, must likewise be sensible how much they wrong themselves, who carry on thoughts of a scrupulous examination and immoderate fears, even to the foot of the altar, and scarce for a short moment have their minds at liberty to think of this better part. It is a weakness and I hope God will forgive it; but certainly they are great losers by it.

When the Christian has taken pains and time thus to prepare his soul, and it is now time to draw near to the altar, he lays whatever can be a hinderance to himself or others, as hat, sword, gloves, etc., and then with a suitable composure of mind and body goes up; and having expressed a reverence to the altar of God, kneels down, and takes the linen cloth. When the *Confiteor* is saying, humbly bowing down he joins with him in the confession of his great unworthiness. When the *Absolution* is given, in the spirit of contrition he desires it may be to him the forgiveness of all the remains of sin. When the priest turns to him with the blessed sacrament in his hands saying '*Domine non sum dignus*: Lord, I am not worthy shouldest thou enter under my roof; say but a word, and my soul shall be healed', he ought to bow down with the humility of the Centurion, and then let a sincere confidence in God follow his distrust in himself. Then kneeling upright, with his mouth moderately opened, he is to receive the blessed sacrament on his tongue, and quickly swallow it down, without bending his head, or raising the towel to his lips.

This whole action he is to perform with great composure of mind, with his heart fixt on God by faith, hope and love; and when the towel is taken away, he is then to turn again to his place, there to give thanks. And here now he is to turn his whole thought to that divine guest whom he has within his breast; he is to entertain him with his most hearty thanks; he is to admire and praise his infinite goodness in coming to visit so poor and unworthy a creature; he is to represent to him all his infirmities, then offer his petitions to him, that he will please to heal his wounds, give him strength for overcoming all his weaknesses, give him patience under all his troubles, confirm and establish him against all assaults of corrupt nature, the devil, and the world, and for being faithful in every duty. Here again he is to renew all his resolutions and beg grace for the exact execution of them. Finally he is to beseech him not to depart without leaving the blessing of a manifest grace behind him. This exercise, for such as are able, is best performed without the help of books, which others, however, are encouraged to use who cannot do so well without them.

But as for those, who after communion huddle over a few prayers in haste, turning their backs upon the altar, presently leave the place, this seems the ready means to lose the benefit of all they have done; for it betrays so little a sense of God's mercy to them, that little can be hoped of fruit from those barren hearts, which, like bare rocks, throw off the seed that falls upon them. Extraordinary accidents, or pressing business, may sometimes break off this exercise, but those who understand their duty, soon contrive some opportunity for taking it up again. Bating such accidents, haste ought to be no where allowed; and if any have this ill custom, it will be a seasonable charity in such as observe it, to give a hint of it to those who may put them upon a better method.

# Personally present
# Thomas More

*Thomas More (1478–1535) wrote several works while he was imprisoned in the Tower of London before his execution, notably the moving* Dialogue of Comfort against Tribulation. *More, as is well known, had been Lord Chancellor, a leader of the new learning championed by Erasmus, reckoned by his contemporaries a witty writer and by posterity as a brilliant contriver of the fantastic Utopia. He resigned his office over Henry VIII's divorce and refused to take the Oath of Supremacy. The short work from which the passage below is taken was written in the Tower in 1534 and was entitled* A treatise to receive the blessed body of our lord sacramentally and virtually bothe. *It is a tranquil work for a man who feared torture even while he trusted God.*

Now when we have receved our lord and have him in our bodye, let us not then let him alone, and geat us furth aboute other thinges, and looke no more unto him (for little good could he, that so would serve any geast), but let all our businesse be about him. Let us by devout prayer talke to him, by devout meditacion talke with him.

Let us say with the prophete: *Audiam quid loquatur in me dominus*, I will heare what our lord will speake within me.

For surely if we set asyde all other thinges, and attend unto him, he will not fayle with good inspirations, to speake suche thinges to us within us, as shal serve to the great spiritual coumfort and profite

169

of our soule. And therfore let us with Martha provide, that al our outward businesse maye be perteyning to him, in makyng chere to him, and to his companye for his sake: that is to wit, to poore folke, of whiche he taketh every one, not only for his disciple, but also as for himselfe. For himself sayth: *Quamdiu fecistis uni de hiis fratribus meis minimis, mihi fecistis.* That that you have done to one of the leaste of these my brethren, you have done it to my self. And let us with Mary also sit in devout meditacion, and hearken we what our savior, being now our geast, wil inwardly say unto us. Nowe have we a speciall time of prayer, whyle he that hath made us, he that hath bought us, he whom we have offended, he that shall judge us, he that shall either damne us or save us, is of his gret goodnes become our geast, and is personallye present within us, and that for none other purpose, but to be sewed unto for pardon, and so thereby to save us. Let us not lese this tyme therfore, suffer not this occasion to slip, whiche we can little tell whether ever we shall geat it agayn or never. Let us endevor our self to kepe him still, and let us say with his two disciples that wer going to the castel of Emaus: '*Mane nobiscum domine,* Tarye with us good lord', and then shall we be sure, that he wil not go from us, but if we unkindly put him from us.

## 34

# The funambulous track
# Thomas Browne

*Sir Thomas Browne (1605–82) was a physician by calling and his best-known book is* Religio Medici. *His eirenic disposition to all Christians sometimes strays towards indifference to belief, and he often seems content to follow the pattern of 'Aristotle's true Gentleman' instead of 'St Paul's noble Christian'. Yet he works in prose what others attempted in verse, by mixing striking images with pleasing cadences to lodge his thoughts easily in our minds.*

*The reflections on virtue here are from* A Letter to a Friend. *The punctuation does not follow modern conventions, but if the reader carries on until a full stop is reached the meaning opens itself up. Browne usually makes clear his harder words and references by saying the same thing again in different words. In the following it is useful to know that Cebes was a friend of Socrates to whom the supposititious* Table *or* Pinax *was attributed; that Origen was said to have castrated himself; that the Trisagium is 'Holy, holy, holy'; and that the Sun in Capricorn is when the days are shortest.*

Tread softly and circumspectly in this funambulous Track and narrow Path of Goodness: pursue Virtue virtuously; be sober and temperate, not to preserve your Body in a sufficiency to wanton Ends; not to spare your Purse; not to be free from the Infamy of common Transgressors that way, and thereby to ballance or palliate obscure and closer Vices; nor simply to enjoy Health: by all which you may leaven good Actions, and render Virtues disputable: but in one Word, that you may truly serve God; which every Sickness will tell you, you cannot well do without Health.

The sick man's Sacrifice is but a lame Oblation. Pious Treasures laid up in healthful days excuse the defect of sick Non-performances; without which we must needs look back with Anxiety upon the lost opportunities of Health; and may have cause rather to envy than pity the Ends of penitent Malefactors, who go with clear parts unto the last Act of their Lives; and in the integrity of their Faculties return their Spirit unto God that gave it.

Consider whereabout thou art in *Cebes* his Table, or that old philosophical Pinax of the Life of Man; whether thou art still in the Road of Uncertainties; whether thou hast yet entred the narrow Gate, got up the Hill and asperous way which leadeth unto the House of Sanity, or taken that purifying Potion from the hand of sincere Erudition, which may send thee clear and pure away unto a virtuous and happy Life.

In this virtuous Voyage let not disappointment cause Despon-

171

dency, nor difficulty Despair: think not that you are sailing from *Lima* to *Manillia*, wherein thou may'st tye up the Rudder and sleep before the Wind; but expect rough Seas, Flaws, and contrary Blasts; and 'tis well if by many cross Tacks and Verings thou arrivest at thy Port. Sit not down in the popular Seats and common Level of Virtues, but endeavour to make them Heroical. Offer not only Peace-Offerings but Holocausts unto God. To serve him singly to serve our selves, were too partial a piece of Piety, nor likely to place us in the highest Mansions of Glory.

He that is chaste and continent not to impair his Strength, or terrified by Contagion, will hardly be heroically virtuous. Adjourn not that Virtue unto those Years when *Cato* could lend out his Wife, and impotent Satyrs write Satyrs against Lust: but be chaste in thy flaming days, when *Alexander* dared not trust his Eyes upon the fair Daughters of *Darius*, and when so many Men think there is no other way but *Origen's.*

Be charitable before Wealth makes thee covetous, and lose not the Glory of the Mite. If Riches increase, let thy Mind hold pace with them; and think it not enough to be liberal, but munificent. Tho a Cup of cold Water from some hand may not be without its Reward; yet stick not thou for Wine and Oyl for the Wounds of the distressed: and treat the Poor as our Saviour did the Multitude, to the Relicks of some Baskets.

Trust not to the Omnipotency of Gold, or say unto it, Thou art my Confidence: kiss not thy Hand when thou beholdest that terrestrial Sun, nor bore thy Ear unto its Servitude. A Slave unto Mammon makes no Servant unto God: Covetousness cracks the Sinews of Faith, numbs the Apprehension of any thing above Sense, and, only affected with the certainty of things present, makes a peradventure of Things to come; lives but unto one World, nor hopes but fears another; makes our own Death sweet unto others, bitter unto our selves; gives a dry Funeral, Scenical Mourning, and no wet Eyes at the Grave.

If Avarice be thy Vice, yet make it not thy Punishment: miserable Men commiserate not themselves, bowelless unto others,

172

and merciless unto their own Bowels. Let the fruition of Things bless the possession of them, and take no satisfaction in dying but living rich: for since thy good Works, not thy Goods, will follow thee; since Riches are an Appurtenance of Life, and no dead Man is rich, to famish in Plenty, and live poorly to dye rich, were a multiplying improvement in Madness, and Use upon Use in Folly.

Persons lightly dip'd, not grain'd in generous Honesty, are but pale in Goodness, and faint hued in Sincerity: but be thou what thou virtuously art, and let not the Ocean wash away thy Tincture: stand magnetically upon that Axis where prudent Simplicity hath fix'd thee, and let no Temptation invert the Poles of thy Honesty: and that Vice may be uneasie, and even monstrous unto thee, let iterated good Acts, and long-confirmed Habits, make Virtue natural, or a second Nature in thee. And since few or none prove eminently virtuous but from some advantageous Foundations in their Temper and natural inclinations; study thy self betimes, and early find, what Nature bids thee to be, or tells thee what thou may'st be. They who thus timely descend into themselves, cultivating the good Seeds which Nature hath set in them, and improving their prevalent Inclinations to Perfection, become not Shrubs, but Cedars in their Generation; and to be in the form of the best of the Bad, or the worst of the Good, will be no satisfaction unto them.

Let not the Law of thy Country be the *non ultra* of thy Honesty, nor think that always good enough which the Law will make good. Narrow not the Law of Charity, Equity, Mercy; joyn Gospel Righteousness with Legal Right; be not a meet *Gamaliel* in the Faith; but let the Sermon in the Mount be thy *Targum* unto the Law of *Sinai*.

Make not the Consequences of Virtue the Ends thereof: be not beneficent for a Name or Cymbal of Applause, nor exact and punctual in Commerce, for the Advantages of Trust and Credit, which attend the Reputation of just and true Dealing; for such Rewards, tho unsought for, plain Virtue will bring with her, whom all Men honour, tho they pursue not. To have other bye ends in good Actions, sowers laudable Performances, which must have deeper Roots, Motions, and Instigations, to give them the Stamp of Virtues.

Tho human infirmity may betray thy heedless days into the popular ways of Extravagancy, yet let not thine own depravity, or the torrent of vicious Times, carry thee into desperate Enormities in Opinions, Manners, or Actions: if thou hast dip'd thy foot in the River, yet venture not over *Rubicon*; run not into Extremities from whence there is no Regression, nor be ever so closely shut up within the holds of Vice and Iniquity as not to find sortie Escape by a Postern of Recipiscency.

Owe not thy Humility unto Humiliation by Adversity, but look humbly down in that State when others look upward upon thee: be patient in the Age of Pride and days of Will and Impatiency, when Men live but by Intervals of Reason, under the Sovereignty of Humor and Passion, when 'tis in the Power of everyone to transform thee out of thy self, and put thee into the short Madness. If you cannot imitate *Job*, yet come not short of *Socrates* and those patient Pagans who tired the Tongues of their Enemies, while they perceiv'd they spet their Malice at brazen Walls and Statues.

Let Age, not Envy, draw Wrinkles on thy Cheeks: be content to be envied, but envy not. Emulation may be plausible, and Indignation allowable; but admit no Treaty with that Passion which no Circumstance can make good. A Displacency at the good of others, because they enjoy it, altho we do not want it, is an absurd Depravity, sticking fast unto humane Nature from its primitive Corruption; which he that can well subdue, were a Christian of the first Magnitude, and for ought I know, may have one foot already in Heaven.

While thou so hotly disclaimst the Devil, be not guilty of Diabolism; fall not into one Name with that unclean Spirit, nor act his Nature whom thou so much abhorrest; that is, to accuse, calumniate, backbite, whisper, detract, or sinistrously interpret others; degenerous Depravities and narrow-minded Vices, not only below *St Paul's* noble Christian, but *Aristotle's* true Gentleman. Trust not with some, that the Epistle of *St James* is Apocryphal, and so read with less fear that stabbing truth, that in company with this Vice thy Religion is in vain. *Moses* broke the Tables without breaking of the Law; but where Charity is broke the Law it self is shattered, which cannot be whole without Love, that is the fulfilling of it. Look humbly upon thy Virtues, and tho thou art rich in some, yet think thy self poor and naked without that crowning Grace, which thinketh no Evil, which envieth not, which beareth, believeth, hopeth, endureth all things. With these sure Graces, while busie Tongues are crying out for a drop of cold Water, Mutes may be in Happiness, and sing the *Trisagium* in Heaven.

Let not the Sun in Capricorn go down upon thy Wrath, but write thy Wrongs in Water; draw the Curtain of Night upon Injuries; shut them up in the Tower of Oblivion, and let them be as tho they had not been. Forgive thine Enemies totally, and without any Reserve of hope, that however, God will revenge thee.

Be substantially great in thy self, and more than thou appearest unto others; and let the World be deceived in thee, as they are in the Lights of Heaven. Hang early Plummets upon the Heels of Pride, and let Ambition have but an Epicycle or narrow Circuit in thee. Measure not thy self by thy Morning shadow, but by the Extent of thy Grave; and reckon thy self above the Earth by the Line thou must be contented with under it. Spread not into boundless Expansions either of Designs or Desires. Think not that Mankind liveth but for a few, and that the rest are born but to serve the Ambition of those, who make but Flies of Men, and Wildernesses of whole Nations. Swell not into Actions which embroil and confound the Earth; but be one of those violent ones which force the Kingdom of Heaven.

# Bird of paradise
# Cotton Mather

*Cotton Mather (1663–1728) was a prominent New England Puritan minister, the son of Increase Mather (1639–1723), whose own father had*

*arrived in Boston in 1635 and had been one of the translators of the popular*
Bay Psalm Book *(1640). Cotton Mather's attitude to witchcraft has been
blamed by some for encouraging the witchcraft trials of 1692. After Increase
Mather had been ousted as President of Harvard, Cotton Mather encouraged
Elihu Yale to support the founding of a new college.*

*Cotton Mather wrote the epitaph below on the death of Shubael Dummer,
the pastor of York, Maine, who was shot dead by Indians during a raid in
January 1692. Increase Mather had written* A Brief History of the Warr
with the Indians *in 1676. The casting of the Indians as devils in the epitaph
for Dummer is uncomfortable; perhaps it helps to compare it to the description
by Aelfric of those who martyred St Edmund, or the attitude towards the pagan
Vikings at the Battle of Maldon in 991 (see p. 190).*

*The language of the epitaph is reminiscent of the Metaphysicals; both
Donne and George Herbert (see above) had used the bird of paradise as a
figure. The Pelican that feeds its young with its blood is a type of Christ,
mentioned by Thomas Aquinas in his* Adoro te devote *in the thirteenth
century and carved in stone at Corpus Christi College, Oxford.*

## Epitaph

DUMMER, the *Shephard* Sacrific'd
By *Wolves*, because the *Sheep* he Priz'd;
The *Orphans'* Father, Churches' Light,
The *Love* of Heaven, of Hell the *Spite*;
The Countreye's *Gapman*, and the *Face*
That *Shone*, but *Knew* it not, with Grace.

DUMMER, a *Wise man of the East*,
Gone to see JESUS, in His Rest:
Hunted by *Divels*, but Reliev'd
By *Angels*, and on High Reciev'd:
The Martyr'd *Pelican*, who *Bled*,
Rather than Leave the Saints *Unfed*,

DUMMER, the *Bird of Paradise*,
*Shot*, and *Flown* thither in a trice;

176

*Methus'la* Dead, from whence our *Flood*,
Threefold of *Tears and Fears and Blood*;
HERE Left his *Ashes*, and we see,
God's *Temple* thus in Ashes —

LORD, Hear the *Cry of Righteous* DUMMER'S Wounds,
Under thine *Altar*, Rate off those *Hounds*
That Worry thus thy *Flocks*: And let the *Bones*
Of thine ELISHA, over whom our Moans
Are Sigh'd, Inspire the *Life of Zeal* into
The Rest, that have a *Work*, Like *His* to Do.


# 35

## Hope and the lion's paw
## Lancelot Andrewes

*Lancelot Andrewes (1555–1626), Bishop of Winchester, was very learned, knowing fifteen languages and possessing a good knowledge of the Fathers of the Church. He valued the sacraments and pursued a life of prayer. His* Preces privatae *were published posthumously both in the original Greek and in translation; John Henry Newman, as an Anglican of a similar mind to Andrewes, translated them in the nineteenth century. Andrewes liked schemata to work upon, an attitude similar to that of the late scholastics. The passage below comes from his* Pattern of Catechetical Doctrine.

*Of hope*
Now as out of knowledge apprehending God's justice, came fear; so out of the same, apprehending mercy, cometh hope and love.

And as true fear is *timor humilians*, 'joined with humility', so true humility hath joined with it hope, lest it should drive to despair; as

177

in Judas (Matthew 1.5), 'He cast down the pieces of silver in the temple, and departed, and went and hanged himself.'

To hope is to look for God's mercy, which is *porta spei*, 'the gate of hope'; whence all good things come.

### How related to other graces

Faith in respect of our weakness bringeth fear, and in respect of God's mercy bringeth hope. Faith believeth the promise, hope looketh for it; for that may be believed that is not hoped for, as hell.

Fear cometh by the faith of the law, and hope by the faith of the gospel.

### The use of hope

The use of hope is twofold;

> that we rest in hope in this life;
> that we rest not here, but look for a better.

As our life is a sea, hope is compared to an anchor whereby we hold fast; as it is a warfare, our hope is a helmet to save our heads from hurt. As the body liveth *spirando*, so the soul *sperando*; and if it come once *desperare*, then the party is in a miserable case; for *spes vitae immortalis est vita vitae mortalis*, 'the blessedness of this life is only the certainty of the life to come'.

### Rules for hope

In hope three things are to be regarded:

1. We must take heed, that as we went out of ourselves by fear, so we do not by hope return to hope in ourselves, but our hope must be in God: Psalm 39.7 'My hope is in Thee'; I Peter 1.21 'That your faith and hope might be in God'.

2. It must be of things to come; for hope that is seen is no hope (Romans 8.24).

3. The things we hope for must not be looked for with security, as

178

if it were an easy matter to be attained; but (I Corinthians 9.27), we must chasten our bodies and bring them in subjection.

## The nature of hope
In the nature of hope there are,

1. Joy, because we hope for that which is good;
2. Grief, because the good we hope for is delayed; now because *dilatio boni habet rationem mali*: 'the deferring of good is in some kind counted an evil'; therefore our hope cannot be secure. And the remedy of the delay is only patience, as Augustine saith [in Psalm 36] *sustine tu ipsum qui sustinuit te; si sustinuit ille te dum corrigeres vitam malam, sustine tu illum dum coronet vitam bonam*: 'be patient towards Him, Who was patient towards thee; if He was patient with thee till thou didst correct the enormity of thy life, be patient at His delay, until He crown thy life godly spent'; and therefore 'hold fast' (Hebrews 10.23).

Basil compareth the gospel to a net, and fear to be the lead which maketh it sink and keepeth it steady, and hope the cork which keepeth always above; without the lead of fear it would be carried hither and thither, and without the cork of hope it would sink down.

For outward things, or God's temporal gifts, there is a desire lawful when God giveth lawful means to come by them; but we must take heed that we do not *male agendo quarere*: 'seek to get any thing by ill means'.

## Extremes to be avoided in hope
The object of hope is *bonum possibile arduum*: a possible good, hard to obtain.

That good we look and hope for, is 'to come', or else it were no hope; and not only *futurum*, but *arduum*: 'hard to come by; possible, but hard. And from these two come two extremes of hope, which are here forbidden: Presumption and Desperation ...

*The means to hope*

1. Compare the enduring hope of the faithful with the perishing hope of the wicked (Proverbs 11.7): 'The hope of unjust men perisheth.'

2. Mark the examples of others that have hoped and were not deceived (Psalm 22.4): 'Our fathers trusted in Thee; they trusted, and Thou didst deliver them'; for this is the devil's craft, to persuade us that our cause is worse than any man's.

3. Remember what experience we have had of God's mercy (I Samuel 17.37): 'The Lord that delivered me out of the paw of the lion and out of the paw of the bear, He will deliver me out of the hand of this Philistine.'

4. Consider the faithfulness of Him that hath promised, and that His *dicere est facere*, 'His word and deed are all one.'

# Pleasant things in ashes
## Anne Bradstreet

*Anne Bradstreet (1612–72) was born in England, the daughter of Thomas Dudley, steward to the puritan earl of Lincoln. She married at sixteen, and two years later sailed with her husband for Massachusetts Bay. Her poetry served as part of her private devotions (although some was taken to England without her knowledge and published in 1650). Since some of it has a psalmic metre, it may be that she sang it as part of her devotions.*

*Detachment from material possessions was an ideal of both Catholic and Protestant spirituality, but a fire destroying home and personal belongings put Anne Bradstreet on her mettle.*

**Here follows some verses upon the burning of our house July 10th, 1666. Copied out of a loose paper.**

In silent night when rest I took
For sorrow near I did not look.
I wakened was with thund'ring noise
And piteous shrieks of dreadful voice.
That fearful sound of 'Fire!' and 'Fire!'

Let no man know is my desire.
I, starting up, the light did spy,
And to my God my heart did cry
To strengthen me in my distress
And not to leave me succourless.
Then, coming out, beheld a space
The flame consume my dwelling-place.
And when I could no longer look,
I blest His name that gave and took,
That laid my goods now in the dust.
Yea, so it was, and so 'twas just.
It was His own, it was not mine,
Far be it that I should repine;
He might of all justly bereft
But yet sufficient for us left.
When by the ruins oft I past
My sorrowing eyes aside did cast,
And here and there the places spy
Where oft I sat and long did lie:
Here stood that trunk, and there that chest,
There lay that store I counted best.
My pleasant things in ashes lie,
And them behold no more shall I.
Under thy roof no guest shall sit,
Nor at thy table eat a bit.
No pleasant tale shall e'er be told,
Nor things recounted done of old.
No candle e'er shall shine in thee,
Nor bridegroom's voice e'er heard shall be.
In silence ever shall thou lie,
Adieu, Adieu, all's vanity.
Then straight I 'gin my heart to chide,
And did thy wealth on earth abide?
Didst fix thy hope on mould'ring dust?
The arm of flesh didst make thy trust?

Raise up thy thoughts above the sky
That dunghill mists away may fly.
Thou hast an house on high erect,
Framed by that mighty Architect,
With glory richly furnished,
Stands permanent though this be fled.
It's purchased and paid for too
By Him who hath enough to do.
A price so vast as is unknown
Yet by His gift is made thine own;
There's wealth enough, I need no more,
Farewell, my pelf, farewell my store.
The world no longer let me love,
My hope and treasure lies above.

## 36

# The liar scorned
# Richard Allestree

*Richard Allestree (1619–81) has been credited with writing* The Whole
Duty of Man, *which was published anonymously, and several sequels.
Allestree was a student (fellow) of Christ Church, Oxford, when the Civil
War broke out, and he was said to have spirited away the college silver which
the parliamentary forces had locked up in the deanery ready to be carried off as
booty. He fought bravely in the war, but then took holy orders. After the
Restoration he became Provost of Eton.*

The speaking Truth is a common debt we owe to all mankind;
speech is given as the instrument of intercourse and society one with
another, the means of discovering the mind, which otherwise lies
hid and concealed, so that were it not for this, our conversations

would be but the same as of beasts. Now this being intended for the good and advantage of mankind, it is a due to it that it be used to that purpose; but he that lies is so far from paying that debt, that on the contrary he makes his speech the means of injuring and deceiving him he speaks to.

There might much be said to show the several sorts of obligations we lie under to speak truth to all men; but supposing I write to Christians, I need not insist upon any other commands we have on it in Scripture; thus (Ephesians 4.25) the Apostle commands that 'putting away lying they speak every man truth with his neighbour', and again (Colossians 3.9) 'Lie not one to another', and (Proverbs 6.17) a lying tongue is mentioned as one of those things that are abominations to the Lord. Yes, so much doth he hate a lie, that it is not the most pious and religious end that can reconcile him to it; the man that lies though in a zeal to God's glory, shall yet be judged as a sinner (Romans 3.7).

What shall then become of those multitudes of men that lie on quite other ends? Some out of malice, to mischief others; some out of covetousness, to defraud their neighbours; some out of pride, to set themselves out; and some out of fear to avoid danger, or hide a fault. But of a yet stranger sort than all these, are those that do it without any discernible temptation, that will tell lies by way of story, take pleasure in telling incredible things, from which themselves reap nothing but the reputation of impertinent liars

Among these divers kinds of falsehood, Truth is become such a rarity among us, that it is a most difficult matter to find such a man as David describes, (Psalm 15.2) 'that speaketh the truth from the heart'. Men have so glibbed their tongues to lying, that they do it familiarly upon any or no occasion, never thinking that they are observed either by God or man. But they are extremely deceived in both; for there is scarce any sin (that is at all endeavoured to be hid) which is more discernible even to men; they that have a custom of lying, seldom fail (be their memory never so good) at some time or other to betray themselves; and when they do, there is

183

no sort of sin meets with greater scorn and reproach: a liar being by all accounted a title of the greatest infamy and shame.

But as for God, it is madness to hope that all their arts can disguise them from him, who needs none of those casual ways of discovery which men do, but sees the heart, and so knows at the very instant of speaking the falsehood of what is said: and then, by his Title of the God of Truth, is tied, not only to hate, but punish it: and accordingly you see (Revelation 22) that the liars are in the number of those that are shut out of the new Jerusalem; and not only so, but also have their part in the lake that burneth with fire and brimstone. If therefore thou be not of the humour of that unjust judge Christ speaks of (Luke 18.2), who neither feared God nor regarded man, thou must resolve on this part of justice, the putting away lying, which is abhorred by both.

# 37

# Spider-man
# John Bunyan

*John Bunyan (1628–88) regrets in his autobiographical* Grace Abounding to the Chief of Sinners *that he spent time playing children's games and listening to tales at the fireside. But his early experience of storytelling must have had its part in the success of* The Pilgrim's Progress *(1678). Among his many other works, he published in 1686* A Book for Boys and Girls *from which this poem is taken. Like all his works it depicts man as utterly degenerate, but always in reach of the mercy of God.*

## The Sinner and the Spider

SINNER    What black? what ugly crawling thing art thou?
SPIDER    I am a Spider —

SINNER   A Spider, Ay, also a filthy Creature.

SPIDER   Not filthy as thy self, in Name or Feature:
  My Name intailed is to my Creation;
  My Feature's from the God of thy Salvation.

SINNER   I am a Man, and in God's Image made,
  I have a Soul shall neither dye nor fade:
  God has possessed me with humane Reason,
  Speak not against me, lest thou speakest Treason.
  For if I am the Image of my Maker,
  Of Slanders laid on me he is Partaker.

SPIDER   I know thou art a Creature far above me,
  Therefore I shun, I fear, and also love thee.
  But tho thy God hath made thee such a Creature,
  Thou hast against him often play'd the Traitor.
  Thy sin hath fetcht thee down: Leave off to boast;
  Nature thou hast defil'd, God's image lost.
  Yea thou, thy self a very Beast hast made,
  And art become like Grass, which soon doth fade.
  Thy Soul, thy Reason, yea thy spotless State,
  Sin has subjected to th'most dreadful fate.
  But I retain my primitive condition,
  I've all, but what I lost by thy Ambition.

SINNER   Thou venom'd thing, I know not what to call thee,
  The Dregs of Nature surely did befall thee;
  Thou wast made of the Dross, and Scum of all;
  Man hates thee, doth in scorn thee Spider call.

SPIDER   My Venom's good for something, 'cause God made it;
  Thy Sin has spoilt thy Nature, doth degrade it
  Of humane Vertues; therefore tho I fear thee,
  I will not, tho I might, despise and jear thee.
  Thou sayst I am the very Dregs of Nature,
  Thy Sin's the spawn of Devils, 'tis no Creature.
  Thou sayst man hates me, 'cause I am a Spider,
  Poor man, thou at thy God art a Derider:
  My venom tendeth to my Preservation;

185

Thy pleasing Follies work out thy Damnation.
Poor man, I keep the rules of my Creation;
Thy sin has cast thee headlong from thy Station.
I hurt no body willingly; but thou
Art a self-Murderer: Thou knowst not how
To do what good is, no thou lovest evil;
Thou fly'st God's Law, adherest to the Devil.

SINNER    Ill-shaped Creature there's Antipathy
'Twixt Men and Spiders, 'tis in vain to lie,
I hate thee, stand off, if thou dost come nigh me,
I'll crush thee with my foot; I do defie thee.

SPIDER    They are ill shap't, who warped are by sin;
Antipathy in thee hath long time bin
To God. No marvel then, if me his Creature
Thou dost defie, pretending Name and Feature.
But why stand off? My Presence shall not throng thee,
'Tis not my venom, but thy sin doth wrong thee.
Come I will teach thee Wisdom, do but hear me.
I was made for thy profit, do not fear me.
But if thy God thou wilt not hearken to,
What can the Swallow, Ant, or Spider do?
Yet will I speak, I can but be rejected;
Sometimes great things, by small means are effected.
Hark then; the man is noble by Creation,
He's lapsed now to such Degeneration;
Is so besotted, and so careless grown,
As not to grieve, though he has overthrown
Himself, and brought to Bondage every thing
Created, from the Spider to the King.
This we poor Sensitives do feel and see;
For subject to the Curse you made us be.
Tread not upon me, neither from me go;
'Tis man which has brought all the world to Woe.
The Law of my Creation bids me teach thee,
I will not for thy Pride to God impeach thee.

186

I spin, I weave, and all to let thee see,
Thy best performances but Cob-webs be.
Thy Glory now is brought to such an Ebb,
It doth not much excel the Spider's Web.
My Webs becoming snares and traps for Flies,
Do set the wiles of Hell before thine eyes.
Their tangling nature is to let thee see,
Thy sins (too) of a tangling nature be.
My Den, or Hole, for that 'tis bottomless,
Doth of Damnation shew the Lastingness.
My lying quat, until the Fly is catcht,
Shews, secretly Hell hath thy ruin hatcht.
In that I on her seize, when she is taken,
I shew who gathers whom God hath forsaken.
The Fly lies buzzing in my Web to tell
Thee, how the Sinners roar and howl in Hell.
Now since I shew thee all these Mysteries,
How canst thou hate me; or me Scandalize?
SINNER    Well, well, I no more will be a Derider;
    I did not look for such things from a Spider.
SPIDER    Come, hold thy peace, what I have yet to say,
    If heeded, help thee may another day.
    Since I an ugly ven'mous Creature be,
    There is some Semblance 'twixt vile Man and Me.
    My wild and heedless Runnings, are like these
    Whose ways to ruin do their Souls expose.
    Day-light is not my time, I work i'th' night,
    To shew, they are like me who hate the Light.
    The slightest Brush will overthrow my house,
    To shew false Pleasures are not worth a Louse.
    The Maid sweeps one Web down, I make another,
    To shew how heedless one's Convictions smother.
    My Web is no defence at all to me,
    Nor will false Hopes at Judgement be to thee.

SINNER   O Spider I have heard thee, and do wonder,
A Spider should thus lighten, and thus thunder ...
SPIDER     I am a Spider, yet I can possess
The Palace of a King, where Happiness
So much abounds. Nor when I do go thither,
Do they ask what, or whence I come, or whither
I make my hasty Travels, no not they;
They let me pass, and I go on my way.
I seize the Palace, do with hands take hold
Of Doors, of locks, or bolts; yea I am bold,
When in, to Clamber up unto the Throne,
And to possess it, as if 'twere mine own.
Nor is there any Law forbidding me
Here to abide, or in this Palace be.
Yea, if I please I do the highest Stories
Ascend, there sit, and so behold the Glories
My self is compast with, as if I were
One of the chiefest Courtiers that be there.
Here Lords and Ladies do come round about me,
With grave Demeanor: Nor do any flout me,
For this my brave Adventure, no not they;
They come, they go, but leave me there to stay.
Now, my Reproacher, I do by all this
Shew how thou may'st possess thy self of Bliss:
Thou art worse than a Spider, but take hold
On Christ the Door, thou shalt not be controul'd.
By him do thou the Heavenly Palace enter,
None chide thee will for this thy brave Adventure.
Approach thou then unto the very Throne,
There speak thy mind, fear not, the Day's thine own.
Nor Saint nor Angel will thee stop or stay;
But rather tumble blocks out of thy way.
My Venom stops not me, let not thy Vice
Stop thee; possess thy self of Paradice.
Go on, I say, although thou be a Sinner,

Learn to be bold in Faith of me a Spinner.
This is the way the Glories to possess,
And to enjoy what no man can express.
Sometimes I find the Palace door up lock't;
And so my entrance thither as up blockt.
But am I daunted? No. I here and there
Do feel, and search; so, if I anywhere,
At any chink or crevise find my way,
I croud, I press for passage, make no stay;
And so, tho difficultly, I attain
The Palace, yea the Throne where Princes reign.
I croud sometimes, as if I'd burst in sunder;
And art thou crush't with striving do not wonder.
Some scarce get in, and yet indeed they enter;
Knock, for they nothing have that nothing venture.
Nor will the King himself throw dirt on thee,
As thou hast cast Reproaches upon me.
He will not hate thee, O thou foul Backslider!
As thou didst me, because I am a Spider.
Now, to conclude; since I such Doctrine bring,
Slight me no more, call me not ugly thing.
God Wisdom hath unto the Piss-ant given,
And Spiders may teach men the way to Heaven.

SINNER   Well, my good Spider, I my Errors see,
I was a fool for railing upon thee.
Thy Nature, Venom, and thy fearful Hue,
Both shew what Sinners are, and what they do.
Thy way and works do also darkly tell,
How some men go to Heaven, and some to Hell.
Thou art my Monitor, I am a Fool;
They learn may, that to Spiders go to School.

## Prayer in battle
## Byrhtnoth

*Byrhtnoth (c. 926–91) was the English commander at the Battle of Maldon, fought in Essex in AD 991 against the heathen Vikings. This is the prayer attributed to him in the anonymous Old English poem about the battle. He uttered it when he was no longer able to stand firmly on his feet just before he was killed in the field with the men who stood by him.*

I thank you, Lord of Hosts, for all the joys which I have known in this world. Now, O merciful Creator, my greatest need is that you should grant grace to my spirit, that my soul might journey to you in your dominion and travel with your protection, O Lord of Angels. I beg you not to let the fiends of hell pull me down.

## 38

## Safer to forget
## Charles Williams

*Charles Williams (1886–1945) worked for Oxford University Press, and wrote poetry, novels and works of literary criticism. A convinced member of the Anglican Church, he strove to explain to others his ruling ideas of romantic love (a kind of love that was personal rather than sloppy) and of the 'coinherence' of all people – a sort of communion of saints by which, for example, others' sufferings can be borne willingly. When the Press was evacuated to Oxford, C. S. Lewis had the opportunity to bring Williams to a wider audience.*

In matters of forgiveness, as in all other virtues (and some vices) the first step is comparatively simple compared to the second. Hell is always waiting for the rebound. The only prevention of the rebound is perseverance. The first moment of forgiveness is nearly always confused with other things – with affection, with delight, with honour, with pride, with love of power; some good, some bad, all distracting. It will happen, often enough, that the forgiveness is rather an emanation of these things than a power in itself. But then, directly afterwards, the good elements will withdraw themselves, and leave the reconciliation to its own serious energy; and if that energy is too weak, it will break; but it will not break alone, for the affection and the joy will be hurt too. Or else the evil elements, the pride and the sense of power, will dominate the reconciliation, and it will become egotistical and a false illusion of the good. Even the light courtesies and settings-aside of our first division need sometimes a second shrug: nothing is achieved at once.

> The horse is taught his manage, and no star
> Of wildest course but treads back his own steps;
> For the spent hurricane the air provides
> As fierce a successor; the tide retreats
> But to return out of its hiding-place
> In the great deep; all things have second birth.

The virtues, however wild their course, have to tread back their own steps; they have, young and innocent, to be taught their manage. They have to learn to be always ready when they are called on; so, they may in time, but only in time, be ready without the calling; their obedience to time and place in us sets them there outside those conditions in the end: 'servitude and freedom are one and interchangeable'.

It is in relation to this management that a footnote may be useful: a footnote on reconciliation. There are two methods of reconciliation: that which remembers the injury in love and that which forgets the injury in love. It is a delicate technique of pardon which can distinguish and (without self-consciousness) use either. Either may be desirable here and now, though there can, of course, be no question which is finally desirable and even necessary to the existence of the Blessed City. There (its architect told us and all its architecture maintains) all things are to be known. We had better not forget it; but even so, 'he that believeth shall not make haste'. Oblivion – say, perfect seclusion of the injury in God – is often here a safer means.

It is often likely that to remember the injury would lead only to some opposite injury. Even the best-intentioned Christians are not always at ease in these sublime states. The mutual act of forgiveness can, too often and too quickly, become a single memory of the sin; the single memory a monstrous interior repetition of recollection; the monstrosity a boredom; the boredom a burden. Or, worse, the sense of superiority is too easily involved. We may say and think we have forgiven and then find we have not; or, worse again, think we have forgiven, and in that self-deception never find that we have not; we may die supposing ourselves to be kindly and self-pleasingly and virtuously reconciled – 'And then will I profess unto them, I never knew you; depart from me, ye that work iniquity.' But also we may in fact have forgiven – say, half-forgiven; and the pardon is thought to free the pardoner to every claim and compel the pardoned to every obedience. 'Such', wrote Blake,

> ... is the Forgiveness of the Gods, the Moral Virtues of the
> Heathen, whose tender Mercies are Cruelty. But Jehovah's
>    Salvation
> Is without Money and without Price, in the Continual
>    Forgiveness of Sins,
> In the Perpetual Mutual Sacrifice in Great Eternity: for behold,
> There is none that liveth and sinneth not.

If it is forbidden to us to demand as a condition of our forgiveness any promise that the offence shall not be repeated, if when he conceded to us the declaration of reconciled love, God retained that condition to himself alone, how much more is it forbidden us to make any other claims, to expect an extra kindness, to ask for an extra indulgence. And how all but impossible to avoid! Forgiving or forgiven, we can claim nothing, at the same time that we have, in God, a right to claim everything. Conceding the permission to promulgate, he conceded also the right to demand; in the Church such things happen. In sacramental confession itself it is the priest who (conditions fulfilled) cannot refuse absolution. Nor we forgiveness; the sinner has all the advantages, as the just son of the prodigal's father felt. But, so admitting, we can slide into an evil mutuality: how easy to claim consideration in return; or if not to claim, at least to expect; or if not to expect, at least to feel we have a right to – somewhere, somehow, some right! Alas, none but what our injurer, of free choice, gives us. Otherwise, the mutuality itself becomes diseased; it grows corrupt with the dreadful stench of the old man on the new way. To forget the sin is the safer method.

# 39

## God is friendship
## Aelred of Rievaulx

*Aelred of Rievaulx (1109–66) came from a northern English family that for three generations had helped preserve the relics of St Cuthbert at Durham. He spent part of his youth at the court of the king of Scotland, and in 1134 joined the new monastery at Rievaulx in Yorkshire, one of the foundations of the growing Cistercian family of Benedictine monks. From 1147 he was its abbot.*

*In his writings he shows something of the new humanism of an era that prefigured the Renaissance, as well as a sincere commitment to the ideals of holiness that he recognized as the aim of monastic life. No fool when it came to dealing with the realities of community life, Aelred in his* Spiritual Friendship *(De Spirituali Amicitia, written as a dialogue) elevates the classical pagan analysis of friendship to a Christian idea of how it participates in a relationship with God: 'You and I, and I hope a third, Christ, in our midst'. Indeed in a daring insight into the life of the Blessed Trinity, Aelred adapts the formula 'God is love' to 'God is friendship'.*

AELRED  Worldly friendship, which is born of a desire for temporal advantage or possessions, is always full of deceit and intrigue; contains nothing certain, nothing constant, nothing secure for, to be sure, it ever changes with fortune and follows the purse. Hence it is written: 'He is a fair-weather friend, and he will not abide in the day of your trouble.' Take away his hope of profit, and immediately he will cease to be a friend. This type of friendship the following lines very aptly deride:

> A friend, not of the man, but of his purse is he,
> Held fast by fortune fair, by evil made to flee.

And yet, the beginning of this vicious friendship leads many individuals to a certain degree of true friendship: those, namely, who at first enter into a compact of friendship in the hope of common profit while they cherish in themselves faith in baneful riches, and who, in so far as human affairs are concerned, reach an acme of pleasing mutual agreement. But a friendship ought in no wise be called true which is begun and preserved for the sake of some temporal advantage.

For spiritual friendship, which we call true, should be desired, not for consideration of any worldly advantage or for any extrinsic cause, but from the dignity of its own nature and the feelings of the human heart, so that its fruition and reward is nothing other than itself.

Whence the Lord in the Gospel says: 'I have appointed you that you should go, and should bring forth fruit', that is, that you should love one another. For true friendship advances by perfecting itself, and the fruit is derived from feeling the sweetness of that perfection. And so spiritual friendship among the just is born of a similarity in life, morals and pursuits, that is, it is a mutual conformity in matters human and divine united with benevolence and charity.

194

Indeed, this definition seems to me to be adequate for representing friendship. If, however, 'charity' is, according to our way of thinking, named in the sense that friendship excludes every vice, then 'benevolence' expresses the feeling to love which is pleasantly roused interiorly.

Where such friendship exists, there, indeed, is a community of likes and dislikes, the more pleasant in proportion as it is more sincere, the more agreeable as it is more sacred; those who love in this way can will nothing that is unbecoming, and reject nothing that is expedient.

Surely, such friendship prudence directs, justice rules, fortitude guards, and temperance moderates. But of these matters we shall speak in their place. Now, then, tell me whether you think enough has been said about the matter you first brought up, namely, the nature of friendship.

IVO Your explanation is certainly sufficient, and nothing else suggests itself to me for further enquiry. But before we go on to other things, I should like to know how friendship first originated among men. Was it by nature, by chance or by necessity of some kind? Or did it come into practice by some statute or law imposed upon the human race, and did practice then commend it to man?

AELRED At first, as I see it, nature itself impressed upon the human soul a desire for friendship, then experience increased that desire, and finally the sanction of the law confirmed it. For God, supremely powerful and supremely good, is sufficient good unto himself, since his good, his joy, his glory, his happiness, is himself.

Nor is there anything outside himself which he needs, neither man, nor angel, nor heaven, nor earth, nor anything which these contain. To him every creature proclaims: 'You are my God, for you have no need of my goods.' Not only is he sufficient unto himself, but he is himself the sufficiency of all things: giving simple being to some, sensation to other, and wisdom over and above these

195

to still others, himself the Cause of all being, the Life of all sensation, the Wisdom of all intelligence.

And thus Sovereign Nature has established all natures, has arranged all things in their places, and has discreetly distributed all things in their own times. He has willed, moreover, for so his eternal reason has directed, that peace encompass all his creatures and society unite them; and thus all creatures obtain from him, who is supremely and purely one, some trace of that unity. For that reason he has left no type of beings alone, but out of many has drawn them together by means of a certain society.

Suppose we begin with inanimate creation – what soil or what river produces one single stone of one kind? Or what forest bears but a single tree of a single kind? And so even in inanimate nature a certain love of companionship, so to speak, is apparent, since none of these exists alone but everything is created and thrives in a certain society with its own kind.

And surely in animate life who can easily describe how clear the picture of friendship is, and the image of society and love? And though in all other respects animals are rated irrational, yet they imitate man in this regard to such an extent that we almost believe they act with reason. How they run after one another, play with one another, so express and betray their love by sound and movement, so eagerly and happily do they enjoy their mutual company, that they seem to prize nothing else so much as they do whatever pertains to friendship.

For the angels too divine Wisdom provided, in that he created not one but many. Among them pleasant companionship and delightful love created the same will, the same desire. Assuredly, since one seemed to be superior, the other inferior, there would have been occasion for envy, had not the charity of friendship prevented it. Their multitude thus excluded solitude, and the bond of charity among many increased their mutual happiness.

Finally, when God created man, in order to commend more highly the good of society, he said: 'It is not good for man to be alone: let us make him a helper like unto himself.' It was from no

196

similar, nor even from the same, material that divine Might formed this helpmate, but as a clearer inspiration to charity and friendship he produced the woman from the very substance of the man. How beautiful it is that the second human being was taken from the side of the first, so that nature might teach that human beings are equal and, as it were, collateral, and that there is in human affairs neither a superior nor an inferior, a characteristic of true friendship.

Hence, nature from the very beginning implanted the desire for friendship and charity in the heart of man, a desire which an inner sense of affection soon increased with a taste of sweetness. But after the fall of the first man, when with the cooling of charity concupiscence made secret inroads and caused private good to take precedence over the common weal, it corrupted the splendour of friendship and charity through avarice and envy, introducing contentions, emulations, hates and suspicions because the morals of men had been corrupted.

From that time the good distinguished between charity and friendship, observing that love ought to be extended even to the hostile and perverse, while no union of will and ideas can exist between the good and wicked. And so friendship which, like charity, was first preserved among all by all, remained according to the natural law among the few good. They saw the sacred laws of faith and society violated by many and bound themselves together by a closer bond of love and friendship. In the midst of the evils which they saw and felt, they rested in the joy of mutual charity.

But in those in whom wickedness obliterated every feeling for virtue, reason, which could not be extinguished in them, left the inclination toward friendship and society, so that without companionship riches could hold no charm for the greedy, nor glory for the ambitious, nor pleasure for the sensuous man. There are compacts – even sworn bonds – of union among the wicked which ought to be abhorred. These, clothed with the beautiful name of friendship, ought to have been distinguished from true friendship by law and precept, so that when true friendship was sought, one might not incautiously be ensnared among those other friendships because of some slight resemblance.

Thus friendship, which nature has brought into being and practice has strengthened, has by the power of law been regulated. It is evident, then, that friendship is natural, like virtue, wisdom, and the like, which should be sought after and preserved for their own sake as natural goods. Everyone that possesses them makes good use of them, and no one entirely abuses them.

IVO  May I ask, do not many people abuse wisdom? Those, I mean, who desire to please men through it, or take pride in themselves by reason of the wisdom placed in them or certainly those who consider it a thing that can be sold, just as they imagine there is a source of revenue in piety.

AELRED  Augustine should satisfy you on that point. Here are his words: 'He who pleases himself, pleases a foolish man, because, to be sure, he is foolish who pleases himself.' But the man who is foolish is not wise; and he who is not wise is not wise because he does not possess wisdom. How then does he abuse wisdom who does not even possess it? And so proud chastity is no virtue, because pride itself, which is a vice, makes conformable to itself that which was considered a virtue. Therefore, it is not a virtue, but a vice.

IVO  But I tell you, with your forbearance, that it does not seem consistent to me to join wisdom to friendship, since there is no comparison between the two.

AELRED  In spite of the fact that they are not coequal, very often lesser things are linked with greater, good with better, weaker with stronger. This is particularly true in the case of virtues. Although they vary by reason of a difference in degree, still they are close to one another by reason of similarity. Thus widowhood is near to virginity, conjugal chastity to widowhood. Although there is a great difference between these individual virtues, there is, nevertheless, a conformity in this, that they are virtues. Now, then, conjugal

198

chastity does not fail to be a virtue for the reason that widowhood is superior in continency. And whereas holy virginity is preferred to both, it does not thereby take away the excellence of the others. And yet, if you consider carefully what has been said about friendship, you will find it so close to, even replete with, wisdom, that I might almost say friendship is nothing else but wisdom.

IVO   I am amazed, I admit, but I do not think that I can easily be convinced of your view.

AELRED   Have you forgotten that Scripture says: 'He that is a friend loves at all times'? Jerome also, as you recall, says: 'Friendship which can end was never true friendship.' That friendship cannot even endure without charity has been more than adequately established. Since then in friendship eternity blossoms, truth shines forth, and charity grows sweet, consider whether you ought to separate the name of wisdom from these three.

IVO   What does this all add up to? Shall I say of friendship what John, the friend of Jesus, says of charity: 'God is friendship'?

AELRED   That would be unusual, to be sure, nor does it have the sanction of the Scriptures. But still what is true of charity, I surely do not hesitate to grant to friendship, since 'he that abides in friendship, abides in God, and God in him'. That we shall see more clearly when we begin to discuss its fruition and utility. Now if we have said enough on the nature of friendship in view of the simplicity of our poor wit, let us reserve for another time the other points you proposed for solution.

IVO   I admit that my eagerness finds such a delay quite annoying, but it is necessary since not only is it time for the evening meal, from which no one may be absent, but, in addition, there are the burdensome demands of the other religious who have a right to your care.

# A prayer for friends
## Anselm

*Anselm (1033–1109) was born in Aosta, in northern Italy. As a young man he travelled to join the monastery at Bec, in Normandy, which Lanfranc had made famous for learning. At the age of sixty, Anselm succeeded Lanfranc as Archibishop of Canterbury.*

*Anselm was a penetrating philosopher, following the* dictum fides quaerens intellectum: *faith in search of understanding. His 'Ontological Argument' for the existence of God has intrigued philosophers down the ages. It seems to demonstrate that if it is possible for there to be a God, then God exists. He was happiest in his monastic community 'as an owl is glad when she is in her hole with her chicks'.*

This is thy commandment, that we love one another. O thou that art good as man, as God, as Lord, as friend, as whatsoever thou art, thy humble servant desires to obey this thy commandment. Thou knowest, O Lord, that I am in love with that love which thou commandest. I seek that love, I follow after it, for the sake of it I, thy poor and needy servant, knock and cry out at the door of thy mercy. And in so far as I have already received the sweet alms of thy free bounty, and love all men in thee and for thy sake, though not as I ought, not as I would, I entreat thee to show mercy to all men. Nevertheless, since there are some whose love thy loving-kindness has in a special way more intimately impressed upon my heart, I do more ardently wish them well, and desire more earnestly to pray for them. Very great is thy servant's longing to pray for them, O good God ...

# 40

## The Delectable Mountains
## H. A. Williams

*Harry Williams (born 1919), a fellow of Trinity College, Cambridge, from 1951 to 1969, impressed a generation of undergraduates with his re-examination of what it means to be a Christian. He particularly criticized the attitude which took comfort in following Christianity as a badge, an accomplishment, a personal possession. For himself, he laid aside all pretence. In 1969, aged fifty, he resigned his fellowship and joined the Community of the Resurrection at Mirfield, Yorkshire.*

*The subtitle of his book* Tensions *(1976), from which the passage here comes, is 'Necessary conflicts in life and love'.*

The pilgrim's progress towards the Celestial City is no easy promenade, nor can it be done in some luxury coach of total resignation or complete certainty or perfect knowledge or some absolute dream of a prayer. We have to slog along on foot, and the most taxing thing about the path is neither its roughness nor its steepness but the fact that, as Jesus said, it's so narrow. Indeed it is often a knife-edge.

But for all the conflicts and tensions we mustn't forget the Delectable Mountains from which we see the Celestial City, if only from afar. Bunyan's picture of the Delectable Mountains is one of the most marvellous in *Pilgrim's Progress*. In terms of Bunyan's story the Delectable Mountains had to be one stage on the road, a temporary resting-place reached when Christian's journey was already more than half over, and which was left behind when the time came to move on. But in life, wherever else we are, we are always also on the Delectable Mountains from which we can catch a glimpse of the Celestial City, the city which is the object of our quest because we know somewhere, somehow, that it is the place where we most truly belong. And while our glimpse of the city lasts, we are at rest. The necessary conflicts of our life are for the time being resolved. And we experience a foretaste of their final and permanent resolution.

The Delectable Mountains can take as many forms as there are people. Your own particular experience of them will not be exactly identical with that of anybody else, since you are a unique person with a unique destiny. Obviously therefore we must go not for the particular but for the general; each person will have his own unique experience of the Delectable Mountains, but we must go for the experience which is common to us all. Some of us are married, some aren't. Some of us are capable of intellectual satisfactions, some aren't. To some of us music reveals Reality, to others it doesn't. Some of us take to religion like a duck to water, others (I am one of them) find it all but intolerable. I have known people to whom rowing in an eight is a mystical experience. There is no need to labour the point further. What we need is a description of the Delectable Mountains which is common to everybody, whoever they are and whatever their talents, predilections or circumstances. If people catch a glimpse of their conflicts resolved, what is the universal form of that vision? I suggest that it is laughter.

I mean real laughter at what is seen as inherently funny. What is the test of real laughter? It is the ability to see the funny side of your own situation, the ability to laugh at yourself as well as about other people. Without the ability to laugh at yourself, to find delighted pleasure in the comic aspects of your own character and circumstances, laughter becomes perverted: a superior sneer, a transparent disguise for cynicism and defeat, a defence mechanism to give to others and yourself the impression that you are more at ease and less frightened than in fact you are – committee laughter, cocktail-party laughter, self-consciously Christian laughter: 'We may be dead but by God we can be cheerful.' A man who laughs at himself, who enjoys the fun of being what he is, does not fall into the perversion of laughter. Mirth, like charity, has to begin at home if it is to be genuine.

In one of Christopher Fry's plays an ageing couple talk of decay and mortality. 'Shall we laugh?' asks the man. 'For what reason?' asks the woman. 'For the reason of laughter', is the reply, 'since laughter is surely the surest touch of genius in creation. Would you ever have thought of it? That same laughter, madam, is an irrelevancy which almost amounts to revelation.'

God, we believe, accepts us, accepts all men, unconditionally, warts and all. Laughter is the purest form of our response to God's acceptance of us. For when I laugh at myself I accept myself and when I laugh at other people in genuine mirth I accept them. Self-acceptance in laughter is the very opposite of self-satisfaction or pride. For in laughter I accept myself not because I'm some sort of super-person, but precisely because I'm not. There is nothing funny about a super-person. There is everything funny about a man who thinks he is. In laughing at my own claims to importance or regard I receive myself in a sort of loving forgiveness which is an echo of God's forgiveness of me. In much conventional contrition there is a selfishness and pride which are scarcely hidden. In our desperate self-concern we blame ourselves for not being the super-persons we think we really are. But in laughter we sit light to ourselves. That is why laughter is the purest form of our response to God.

Whether or not the great saints were capable of levitation, I have not the evidence to decide. What I do know is that a characteristic of the great saints is their power of levity. For to sit light to yourself is true humility. Pride cannot rise to levity. As G. K. Chesterton said, pride is the downward drag of all things into an easy solemnity. It would seem that a heavy seriousness is natural to man as falling. 'It was by the force of gravity that Satan fell.' Laughter, on the other hand, is a sign of grace.

Nowhere in all literature is this point put more devastatingly or more poignantly than in *King Lear*. From the start Lear takes himself with the utmost seriousness. His pride makes him utterly blind and leads him to actions, which drive him to insanity and

203

destruction. If only he could see the joke he would be saved. But he can't. Yet the Fool tries continually to make him see it, and Lear's self-imprisonment in a situation where humour is so totally out of place as to be obscene is one of the most horrific aspects of the play. Lear is in hell because he has made laughter loathesomely inappropriate. His egotistical self-dramatization as the most generous of fathers has led two of his daughters to disown him. And he says to the Fool: 'When were you wont to be so full of songs, sirrah?' To which the Fool answers: 'I have used it, nuncle, ever since thou madest thy daughters thy mothers': ever since 'thou gavest them the rod and put'st down thine own breeches'. Or when in madness Lear tears off his clothes, the Fool says: 'Prithee, nuncle, be contented: 'tis a naughty night to swim in.' If in the intolerable grimness of his self-inflicted torture Lear could have risen to the merest flicker of a laugh, he would have been a man redeemed. The pride which from the first has made him incapable of laughter is the essence of his appalling tragedy.

So, from the bottom of your heart thank God when you can see the joke popping out of your circumstances, even when they are grim. Thank God when you can take a delighted pleasure in the comic spectacle, which is yourself, especially if it is yourself devoutly at prayer. Thank God when you can laugh. It means that you are on the Delectable Mountains and that your redemption has drawn nigh.

# 'Come' or 'Go'
# Mother Teresa

*Mother Teresa of Calcutta (1910–97) became known for her work with the poorest of the poor, not as a sort of social service, but as an expression of her conviction that it was Jesus that she found in them, whatever their religion.*

Today the Poor are hungry, for bread and rice – and for love and the living word of Christ.

The Poor are thirsty, for water – and for peace, truth and justice.

The Poor are naked, for clothes – and for human dignity and compassion for the naked sinner.

The Poor are homeless, for a shelter made of bricks – and for a joyful heart that understands, covers, loves.

The Poor are sick, for medical care – and for that gentle touch and a warm smile.

The 'shut-in', the unwanted, the unloved, the alcoholics, the dying destitutes, the abandoned and the lonely, the outcasts and the untouchables, the leprosy sufferers – all those who are a burden to society, who have lost all hope and faith in life, who have forgotten how to smile, who have lost the sensibility of the warm hand-touch of love and friendship – they look to us for comfort.

If we turn our backs on them, we turn it on Christ, and at the hour of our death we will be judged on if we have recognized Christ in them and on what we have done for them and to them. There will be only two ways: 'Come' or 'Go'.

# Sources and further reading

**p. 3** Richard Crashaw. From *Steps to the Temple*. His poetry is in print in hardback (Oxford: Oxford University Press, 1957), or paperback (Sevenoaks: Hodder & Stoughton, 1972), and pleasant editions turn up in second-hand shops for less than new hardbacks.

**p. 7** Lanfranc. From *The Monastic Constitutions*, trans. David Knowles (London: Thomas Nelson, 1951).

**p. 11** George Fox. From *The Journal of George Fox* (London: Headley Bros., 1902; Penguin, 1998). Fox's remarkable *Book of Miracles* is available in paperback (London: Quaker Home Service, 2000).

**p. 18** Christopher Smart. From *The Collected Poems*, ed. Norman Callan, 2 vols (London: Routledge & Kegan Paul, 1949). Oxford University Press is publishing the complete poetry in expensive volumes. Selected poetry is available in Penguin (Harmondsworth, 1990).

**p. 20** Charlotte Bedingfeld. From *The Jerningham Letters*, ed. Egerton Castle, (London: Richard Bentley, 1896).

**p. 29** Francis Quarles. From *Emblems*. A facsimile of the 1635 edition was published by Georg Olms in 1990. Second-hand copies with illustrations tend to be expensive unless in poor condition.

**p. 32** Joseph Butler. From *The Works*, ed. W. E. Gladstone (Oxford: Clarendon Press, 1896). The *Analogy* is easy to find second-hand.

**p. 39** Hannah More. From *Practical Piety* (London, 1824).

**p. 40** Augustine. From *Confessions*, trans. Abraham Woodhead, 1679. Modern translations include those of Henry Chadwick

(Oxford: Oxford Paperback, 1998) and F. J. Sheed (London: Continuum/Sheed & Ward, 1987). The scholarly *Works of St Augustine* in many volumes (New York: New City Press, 1997) is a lively modern translation. Loeb publish a Latin and English facing-pages edition (1912). Frederick van der Meer's *Augustine the Bishop* (London: Sheed & Ward, 1961) gives a vivid picture of him in his time and place.

**p. 44** William Whiting. 'For those in peril on the sea' is included in *Hymns Ancient and Modern* and other collections, including *The English Hymnal*.

**p. 45** William Caxton. From *The Golden Legend* (London: J. M. Dent, 1900). Jacobus de Voragine's *Golden Legend* is translated into modern English by William Granger Ryan (Princeton, NJ: Princeton University Press, 1993).

**p. 48** Alfred the Great. From *Gregory's Pastoral Care in The Whole Works of King Alfred the Great* (Oxford and Cambridge: J. F. Smith, 1852). This hopeless translation does not contain the complete works at all. Alfred's *Pastoral Care* in Old English is published by the Early English Text Society (Woodbridge: Boydell & Brewer, 1996).

**p. 51** Benedict of Nursia. From *The Rule of St Benedict*, trans. D. Oswald Hunter Blair (Fort Augustus: Abbey Press, 1934). There are many modern translations; Justin McCann's version was reissued by Sheed & Ward (London: 1995).

**p. 57** Thomas à Kempis. There are plenty of paperback modern English translations.

**p. 59** Thomas Traherne. From *Poems, Centuries and Three Thanksgivings*, ed. Anne Ridler (Oxford: Oxford University Press, 1966; Greville Paperback, 2000). Penguin has *Selected Poems and Prose*.

207

**p. 63** Alcuin. There is a standard Latin text of Alcuin's poetry in *Poetae Latini Aevi Carolini*, ed. Ernst Dummler (Berlin, 1881). For his life and times see E. Duckett , *Alcuin, Friend of Charlemagne, His World and Work* (1965); Stephen Allott, *Alcuin of York: His Life and Letters* (1974).

**p. 65** John Wesley. From *The Works of John Wesley*, Vol II (London: Wesleyan-Methodist Book Room, n.d., but nineteenth century). There is a scholarly edition of the works in progress, published by Abingdon; vol. 24 is expected in 2003. But the *Journal* and his *Letters* can be found in standard editions second-hand.

**p. 66** Samuel Johnson. The scholarly edition is the expensive *Diaries, Prayers and Annals* (New Haven, CT: Yale University Press, 1958). Second-hand editions of the *Prayers*, together with Johnson's *Sermons*, can be found.

**p. 71** Henry Vaughan. From *The Works of Henry Vaughan*, ed. Leonard Cyril Martin (Oxford: Clarendon, 1914).

**p. 72** Richard Rolle. From a manuscript of *The Form of Perfect Living* (Ms. Rawl. c.285) extracted in *The Coasts of the Country, An Anthology of Prayer drawn from the Early English Spiritual Writers*, ed. and modernized by Clare Kirchberger (London, 1955).

**p. 73** Henry VI. From *Memoir of John Blacman*, ed. M. R. James (Cambridge: Cambridge University Press, 1910).

**p. 74** Pacificus Baker. From *The Christian Advent, or Entertainments for that Holy Season in Moral Reflections and Pious Thoughts and Aspirations* (London, 1755).

**p. 77** Francis of Assisi. From *Saint Francis of Assisi: Omnibus of Sources*, 2 vols (Franciscan Press, Quincy University, 1991). This is still in print.

**p. 78** Bernard of Clairvaux. From what is called a sermon, but is more like an intimate meditation designed to facilitate private prayer. It comes from vol. 3 of *The Life and Works of St Bernard*, ed. Samuel J. Eales, (London: John Hodges, 1896). Eales based his edition on that of the great seventeenth-century scholar Dom John Mabillon of the learned community of St Maur.

**p. 82** Star of the Sea. The Latin text is available very cheaply with a good selection of English and Latin prayers in the *St Paul Prayer Book* (London: St Pauls, 2000). The traditional Gregorian chant music for it and many other Latin hymns and prayers is included in *Liber Cantualis* (Solesmes, Sable-sur-Sarthe; Abbaye Saint-Pierre de Solesmes, 1978), which is still in print and at the lower end of mid-price range. An impressive rendering of the Monteverdi setting is on the CD: *Monteverdi Vespro della Beata Vergine 1610* (The Monteverdi Choir & Orchestra, cond. John Elliot Gardiner, 1972, 1994, Decca, 443 482-2).

**p. 83** Lady Lucy Herbert. From *Several Excellent Methods of Hearing Mass with Fruit and Benefit* (London, 1791).

**p. 87** Robert Southwell. From *Marie Magdalen's Funerall Teares for the Death of our Saviour* (London: Charles Baldwyn, 1823).

**p. 90** Ronald Knox. From *St Paul's Gospel* (London: Sheed & Ward, 1950). Knox's translation of the Bible is easy to find second-hand. So is *Enthusiasm*, in a well-produced hardback edition. It has been republished in paperback. Knox wrote an autobiography called *A Spiritual Aeneid* when he became a Catholic during the First World War. Other successful books include *Let Dons Delight* (1939). Knox was a great stylist and a persuasive analyst. One of his satirical essays proves that Queen Victoria wrote *In Memoriam*. Evelyn Waugh wrote a memoir, *Ronald Knox*, which has a gloomy air.

**p. 99** John Donne. The poetry is in print. Extracts from the sermons in *John Donne: Selected Prose*, ed. Helen Gardiner and T. Healy (London: Oxford University Press, 1967). There is an expensive learned edition of the sermons in ten volumes (Berkeley, CA: University of California Press, 1953–61), which may be obtained from libraries.

**p. 101** Rowan Williams is also the compiler with Geoffrey Rowell and Kenneth Stevenson of *Love's Redeeming Work: The Anglican Quest for Holiness* (Oxford: Oxford University Press, 2001).

**p. 105** *Salve sancta facies.* Anonymous prayer found in Ms. Univ. Coll. clxxix, fol. 14v, modernized by Clare Kirchberger in *The Coasts of the Country: An Anthology of Prayer Drawn from the Early English Spiritual Writers* (London, 1955).

**p. 105** William Sancroft. From *Lex Ignea* (London, 1666). My thanks to Corinna Honan, who kindly lent me her copy.

**p. 110** William Williams and Peter Williams. The hymn has been widely anthologized.

**p. 111** Wiliam Law. From *A Serious Call*, in Vol. 4 of *The Works of the Reverend William Law in Nine Volumes*, printed for J. Richardson, 1762 (privately repr. for G. Moreton, Setley, Hampshire, 1893). I looked at this handsome edition in a library, but Law's *Serious Call* is easily found cheaply in second-hand shops and new in paperback.

**p. 112** Elizabeth I. The prayer is printed, with variants, in *Collected Works* (Chicago, IL: University of Chicago Press, 2000). But this volume does not include Elizabeth's interesting translation of Boethius.

**p. 113** Julian of Norwich. From Chapter 31 of *Revelations of Divine Love Shewed to a Devout Ankress by Name Julian of Norwich*, ed. Dom

Roger Huddleston OSB (London: Burns & Oates, 1927; new edition, 1952). He has partly modernized the text. In more than small doses, the false correspondence between archaic meanings of words and modern meanings can be tiresome. There is a translation by Clifton Walters in Penguin Classics (Harmondsworth, 1966; repr. 1973) but there the reader sometimes wonders exactly what the original wording was (for Julian uses some daring phraseology). An edition in Middle English is published by the Early English Text Sociey (Woodbridge: Boydell & Brewer).

**p. 119** Francis de Sales. From *A Treatise of the Love of God, translated into English by Miles Car* [Miles Pinkney], *Priest of the English Colledge of Doway* (Douay, 1630). Both *The Love of God* and *An Introduction to the Devout Life* were published in the Orchard series by Burns & Oates, and these are easily come by second-hand.

**p. 123** Catechism of Edward VI. From *The Two Liturgies (1549, 1552), with the Order of Communion 1548; The Primer 1553; The Catechism and Articles 1553; the Catechismus Brevis 1553* (Cambridge: The Parker Society, 1844).

**p. 124** John of the Cross. From *The Collected Works of Saint John of the Cross*, trans. Kieran Kavanaugh OCD and Otilio Rodriguez OCD (Washington, DC: Institute of Carmelite Studies, 1991).

**p. 126** George Herbert. From *The English Works of George Herbert* (London, 1905). The poetry is in print and easily available second-hand.

**p. 127** Mark Allen and Ruth Burrows. From *Letters on Prayer* (London: Sheed & Ward, 1999).

**p. 134** Bede. From *The Complete Works of Venerable Bede*, Vol. 4 (London, 1843). Most of these are in Latin. The *Ecclesiastical History* is in translation in various current editions.

**p. 135** George MacDonald. From *Unspoken Sermons, Third Series*. More extracts are included in *George MacDonald: An Anthology*, ed. C. S. Lewis (London: Geoffrey Bles, 1946).

**p. 136** James Barnard. From *The Life of the Venerable and Reverend Richard Challoner DD*, by James Barnard (London, 1784). On the title page Barnard boasted of 'near twenty years' personal acquaintance' with Challoner. Eamon Duffy edited a collection of essays, *Challoner and His Church* (1981). Challoner's *Memoirs of Missionary Priests*, and various of his books of devotions, sometimes much revised, can be found second-hand.

**p. 140** Thomas Ken. From *The Prose Works of Thomas Ken*, ed. Revd W. Benham (London: Griffith, Farren, Okeden & Welsh, 1889).

**p. 144** The Sarum Primer. The prayer is well known from the musical setting by Henry Walford Davies (1869–1941), organist at the Temple Church, London.

**p. 145** *The Cloud of Unknowing*. An edition in Middle English is published by the Early English Text Society. A translation was published by Abbot Justin McCann (London: Burns & Oates, 1924), but it is in pretty strange English.

**p. 148** George Herbert. See note for p. 126.

**p. 150** Teresa of Avila. From Chapter 39 of *The Way of Perfection*. The translation is based on E. A. Peers' edition of her works, with adjustments. Teresa is often ambiguous in phrasing, though her overall drift is unmistakable.

**p. 153** John Henry Newman. From *Prayers, Verses and Devotions* (London: Ignatius Press; repr. 2002). All of Newman's works are available second-hand; the *Apologia Pro Vita Sua*, his compelling autobiography, is particularly easy to find, and is in print in paperback. His *Development of Christian Doctrine* exerted an influence on twentieth-century theology.

**p. 154** Augustine Baker. From *Holy Wisdom, Extracted out of more than Forty Treatises and Methodically Digested by Serenus Cressy* (1657), ed. Abbot Sweeney (London: Burns & Oates, 1911). This was republished in the Orchard Series, and again by A. Clarke Books in 1972.

**p. 158** Edward Taylor. The standard edition is *The Poems of Edward Taylor*, ed. Donald E. Stanford (New Haven, CT: Yale University Press, 1960).

**p. 161** Martin Luther. From *The Table Talk of Martin Luther*, trans. and ed. William Hazlitt (London, 1883). A new multivolume edition of Luther's works in English translation was undertaken by Concordia (St Louis, MO).

**p. 162** Anthony Sparrow. From *A Rationale or Practical Exposition of the Book of Common Prayer* (7th edn; London, 1722).

**p. 164** Ave verum corpus. Available without or with musical notation as in note for page 82, Star of the Sea.

**p. 164** John Gother. From *Afternoon Instructions for Sundays, Holy-Days and Other Feasts*, in *The Spiritual Works of John Gother*, 16 vols (Newcastle, 1792).

**p. 169** Thomas More. From *The Complete Works of St Thomas More*, Vol 13 (New Haven, CT: Yale University Press, 1976). Perhaps the most approachable of More's religious works is the *Dialogue of Comfort against Tribulation*, which can be found second-hand or in libraries.

**p. 170** Thomas Browne. From *Religio Medici and Other Works* (Oxford: Oxford University Press, 1964). The most useful edition of

213

Browne's works is not Geoffrey Keynes's twentieth-century text but Simon Wilkin's nineteenth-century edition (London: Bohn, 1852), which has useful notes. It is to be found second-hand, at a reasonable price for a working copy.

**p. 175** Cotton Mather. The standard edition is *Cotton Mather's Verse in English*, ed. Denise D. Knight (Delaware City, DE: University of Delaware Press, 1989).

**p. 177** Lancelot Andrewes. From *A Pattern of Catechetical Doctrine* (Henry Parker, 1846). Andrewes' sermons were also published by Henry Parker in the 1840s, and can be found second-hand.

**p. 180** Anne Bradstreet. The standard edition is *The Works of Anne Bradstreet*, ed. Jeannine Hensley (Cambridge, MA: Harvard University Press, 1967).

**p. 182** Richard Allestree. From *The Whole Duty of Man* (London, 1842). The book is generally published without attribution, and is easy to find second-hand in various editions.

**p. 184** John Bunyan. From *A Book for Boys and Girls* (1686). *The Pilgrim's Progress* and *Grace Abounding* are in print in paperback. George Offor's big three-volume edition of Bunyan's Works (London, 1862) is useful. Oxford University Press has been issuing expensive volumes of a learned edition. *The Poems*, ed. Graham Midgeley, were published as one volume (Oxford: Oxford University Press, 1980).

**p. 190** Byrhtnoth. A version in Old English with a translation is included in *The Battle of Maldon*, ed. Donald Scragg (Oxford: Basil Blackwell, 1991; paperback, Stroud: Tempus, 2003). Another translation is in *Three Anglo-Saxon Battle Poems* (Llanerch Press, 1996, paperback). An interesting view on J. R. R. Tolkien's attitude to the poem, the heroic ideal and Christianity, comes in

Tom Shippey's *J.R.R. Tolkien: Author of the Century* (London: HarperCollins, 2001).

**p. 190** Charles Williams. From *The Forgiveness of Sins* (London: Geoffrey Bles, 1952).

**p. 193** Aelred of Rievaulx. From *Spiritual Friendship*, trans. Mary Eugenia Laker (Kalamazoo, MI: Cistercian Publications, 1977).

**p. 200** Anselm. *The Prayers and Meditations (with the Proslogion)*, trans. Benedicta Ward, were published by Penguin Classics. *The Major Works*, ed. Brian Davies, are in paperback (Oxford: Oxford World Classics, reissued 1998). The *Life*, by Eadmer, trans. R. W. Southern, was published by Oxford University Press in 1972, and republished by Sandpiper.

**p. 201** Harry Williams. From *Tensions* (London: Mitchell Beazley, 1976). His best-known book, *The True Wilderness* (London: Constable, 1965), was reissued by Mowbrays in 1994.

**p. 204** Mother Teresa. *Mother Teresa of Calcutta: A Fruitful Branch on the Vine* (Saint Anthony Messenger Press, 2000, paperback) has some of Mother Teresa's own words. There are more in *My Life for the Poor*, ed. José Luis Gonzalez-Balado and Janet N. Playfoot (New York: Ballantine Books, 1987). But it is worth checking what has been published recently, since interest continues in this saintly woman.